Kim Revill

111 Places
in Leeds
That You
Shouldn't Miss

Photographs by Alesh Compton

emons:

In memory of Ben Kendrick, one of the kinder people
I met along the way and JB whom I never got the chance to meet.

Bibliographical information of the Deutsche Nationalbibliothek
The Deutsche Nationalbibliothek lists this publication in the
Deutsche Nationalbibliografie; detailed bibliographical data are
available on the internet at http://dnb.d-nb.de.

© Emons Verlag GmbH
All rights reserved
All photographs © Alesh Compton, except:
John Arnison, airestreetdarkroom.com.uk (ch. 15, 17, 18, 24, 30, 35, 43, 61, 82, 86,
87, 89, 110, 111); photographs reproduced by kind permission of 21 Co. (ch. 1):
Ailith Harley-Roberts; Chippendale Collection (ch. 20): Harewood House;
City Varieties Royal Box (ch. 21): The Grand Theatre; Dry Stone Walling (ch. 24):
Martin Longbottom; The Horned Helmet (ch. 38): The Royal Armouries;
Opera North (ch. 77): Opera North; The Otters of Leeds (ch. 80):
www.pixabay.com; The Skyliner (ch. 90): Alvin Meehan; Sound Leisure (ch. 92):
Black Family, Sound Leisure; Sunny Bank Mills (ch. 100): Joanne Crawford (top),
Lorne Campbell (bottom)
© Cover image: mauritius images/Rob Ford/Alamy
Layout: Eva Kraskes, based on a design
by Lübbeke | Naumann | Thoben
Maps: altancicek.design, www.altancicek.de
Basic cartographical information from Openstreetmap,
© OpenStreetMap-Mitwirkende, OdbL
Editing: Rosalind Horton
Printing and binding: Grafisches Centrum Cuno, Calbe
Printed in Germany 2023
ISBN 978-3-7408-2059-6
Revised third edition, October 2023

Guidebooks for Locals & Experienced Travellers
Join us in uncovering new places around the world at
www.111places.com

Foreword

Welcome to the great northern city of Leeds! It is an inclusive, diverse place that welcomes all. Leeds holds an impressive history, and its future is looking bright. Without wishing to make a fuss about it, Leeds has edged quietly up the league table as one of the best places to live or visit in Britain. It is one of the UK's fastest growing cities. There may have been a bit more boasting recently with the celebrations that took place in and around town for Leeds 2023 Year of Culture, during which the city hosted performances, live music, exhibitions, workshops, poetry readings, films and much more.

Leeds is traditionally rich in culture. It is home to the Phoenix Dance Theatre, the Northern Ballet, the Leeds School of Contemporary Dance and Opera North. Channel 4 moved its news studios to the renovated Majestic building in the heart of the city, originally a 1920s cinema, famous later for being a dance hall. The city is renowned for its ornate, beautifully preserved Victorian arcades surrounded by a surprising number of ancient alleyways, nooks and crannies that can lead you to watering holes out of the wind and rain.

Household names such as Marks, Spencer, Burton, Barran and Marshall all started their businesses in Leeds from meagre means. Some were local, but Marks and Burton were refugees, forced to flee from persecution in Eastern Europe simply because of their Jewish heritage. Leeds has produced the great pioneering engineers, such as Smeaton, Blenkinsop and Murray. Smeaton is still known as the 'father of civil engineering', and Blenkinsop and Murray were inventors of the first steam locomotives in the world. Their legacies live on and are woven into the story of Leeds.

Leeds enjoys beautiful countryside on all four compass points, and the city has many places of natural beauty hidden among its urban pockets. So go exploring and enjoy all that Leeds has to offer.

Kim Revill

111 Places

1   21 Co.

Bringing sunshine and smiles to the customers

In 2021, Leeds-born George Webster made British history by becoming the first BBC young children's presenter with Down Syndrome. But George's first big break into employment was cheerfully serving customers at 21 Co., a café and shop in Headingley. His busy schedule permitting, the author, actor and Mencap ambassador pops in from time to time.

21 Co. gives young people with Down Syndrome a decent future by providing the essential skills for a solid footing in the job market. Its very existence aims to challenge often negative perceptions about people with disabilities. The idea for the café and shop was conceived by the Leeds-based charity Sunshine & Smiles, a support network aimed at improving lives of young people and children with Down Syndrome and their families. The 11 young adults employed by 21 Co., aged between 18 and 40, are assigned mentors on the job and paid a living wage. All the profits are ploughed back into the venture, and any surplus cash is happily donated to Sunshine & Smiles.

Hot and cold drinks are served, and customers enjoy beautifully decorated lattes and cappuccinos adorned with the Sunshine & Smiles' happy-face logo. Bakes are locally sourced from Leeds Bread Co-Op, Holy Doughly and Sugar Crush Bakes. The project also offers flowers and gifts, which include cards, jewellery and artwork, mostly sourced from local creatives. A play area filled with an array of colourful books is also provided. The pandemic forced months of closure, but the team rallied round to open the doors once more with the help of some sponsors. More than 1 million young people in the UK live with disabilities, and tackling ableism continues to be a challenge. However, working at the café gave George, already a BAFTA-winning presenter and *Strictly Come Dancing* alumnus, a sense of ambition and a can-do attitude. 'We too can dream big and be employed,' he said.

Address Headingley Central, Unit 32, Otley Road, LS6 2UE, +44 (0)7725 041601, www.21co.org.uk, hello@sunshineandsmiles.org.uk | Getting there Bus 6, 8, 27, 28, 85; by car: take the A 660 Otley Old Road from the city centre | Hours Wed & Thu 9am–2pm, Fri & Sat 9am–4.30pm, Sun 10.30am–4.30pm | Tip Nearby at No. 9 Otley Road is a traditional, family-run, Indian restaurant called De Baga. It is extremely popular with locals and fans who have enjoyed a day's cricket at Headingley Stadium. Booking is highly recommended.

2 840 to Whitby

Voted Britain's most scenic bus ride

Such is the size of the county of Yorkshire, this bus ride from Leeds to Whitby on Yorkshire's northern coast takes three hours to complete, so it is a bit of a pilgrimage. It is not for those with a hectic timetable to keep, but faith and tenacity will definitely pay off.

The 840 Leeds to Whitby was voted Britain's most scenic bus journey in a poll conducted last year and this ride has it in huge buckets and spades, attracting visitors worldwide. Those who are able to climb the stairs on the double decker, are advised to do so to get the best of the views.

Four 840 buses a day make their way from Leeds to the brewery town of Tadcaster before heading to the historic walled city of York and onwards through the green pastures of 'God's Own County'. Passengers have a choice to leave the bus at any of the destinations *en route* but the fishing port of Whitby is the last, and a glorious outpost for the journey's end.

After marvellous York, the bus makes its way to the charming market towns of Malton, Pickering and Thornton-le-Dale in the stunning Dalby Forest. It even makes a detour to the village of Kirby Misperton, the nearest access point to the adventure park Flamingo Land. Passengers can also get to Eden Camp, a World War II museum, courtesy of the 840. Climbing up and over the North York Moors – one of two national parks in Yorkshire – the bus heads into the village of Goathland where you can swap the bus for the steam train on the North Yorkshire Moors Railway. The village is famous for posing as Hogsmeade station in the Harry Potter films and was the setting for the television series, *Heartbeat*.

After leaving Goathland, the bus ascends once again over the heather-peppered moors before excited gasps can be heard on a clear day when the gothic Whitby Abbey finally comes into view. It prompts that most quoted of child-like phrases: 'I can see the seaeeee!'

Address Leeds City Bus Station, Dyer Street, LS2 7LA, +44 (0)1653 692556, www.bustimes.org/services/840-leeds-whitby | Getting there The buses usually leave from stand 21 but it is advisable to check the website | Hours There are four buses a day from Leeds, at 7am, 9.15am, 11.15am & 1.15pm, and five returning from Whitby, at 9am, 11am, 1pm, 3pm & 5.45pm | Tip You can give yourself a fish and chips treat after a long journey by eating at the famous Magpie Café on Pier Street, Whitby, but it is very popular so patience is needed as there may be queues.

3 — Anand Sweets

A remarkable place to eat in Yorkshire

When you look above and beyond the most well-known places in and around Leeds, you will almost certainly be rewarded with the discovery of Anand's Sweets in the suburb of Harehills.

Anand Sweets is a sweet-and-savoury, vegetarian, and vegan café and takeaway founded by Anand Dayal Dadu, who was born and brought up in Hyderabad in southern India's Telangana state. In 1988, he started the brand Anand Sweets in Bengaluru, the capital of Karnataka, with his wife and brother. They opened a branch of the business in Leeds in 2000, as they wanted to appeal to the racially diverse clientele of the city. There is now a branch in the equally diverse area of Hyde Park.

Sweets, also known as *mithai* in Hindi and Urdu, are traditional delicacies, usually served at Indian weddings, religious ceremonies and other celebrations. After a period when Anand handed over to his sons, the Leeds business is now under the ownership of chefs, Surjit Chera and her husband Harvinder, who continue with the name but prepare their own brand of home-cooked foods, such as *kachori chana chat*, *bhel puri* and *dhokla*, all cooked using various types of *ghee*, or clarified butter, giving dishes an authentic Indian taste. They source most of their ingredients from India, but the food is made on the premises.

Customers can try out their speciality *mithais* beautifully presented on the plate or in gift boxes. These sweet treats are usually served alongside a savoury meal, especially in times of celebration. However, they can be eaten any time of the year at the café and washed down by a masala chai.

In 2022, Anand Sweets featured in the BBC programme *Remarkable Places to Eat in Yorkshire*. *Great British Bake Off* winner and chef Nadiya Hussain introduced restaurateur Fred Sirieix to sweet and savoury tastes at Anand, as she was once a regular customer when she lived in Leeds. She described Anand as 'the king of samosas.'

Address 109 Harehills Road, Harehills, LS8 5HS, +44 (0)113 2481234, www.anandsweets.co.uk | Getting there Bus 50, 50A, 49, get off at Conway View; by car: an 8-minute drive via A 58 New York Road / Burmantofts Street / Beckett Street | Hours Tue – Sat 10am – 8pm Sun 10am – 7pm | Tip Nearby on Roundhay Road, another little gem providing a taste of home to the West Indian community, is Maureen's Carribbean Kitchen. This is home cooking at its most authentic. It is a takeaway and tiny restaurant delivering a cultural dining experience.

4 The Back-to-Backs

Still iconic bedrocks of the North

Back-to-back houses were often used as grimy backdrops in northern kitchen sink dramas of the 1960s, where angry young men raged against a system designed to manacle the working classes. Today, some of the back-to-backs and through terraced houses have emerged to become timeless remnants of social history: they have become museum pieces, and scholars have studied them for doctorates. True, many have seen better days, but the high-rise alternatives are often viewed as outdated eyesores and potential death traps.

Almost 70 per cent of Leeds was showered in back-to-back housing prior to World War I. The majority were built primarily for the factory workers, and engineered so that they would be in easy stepping distance to clock-in. Some of the urban cottages, as they were also known, date back as far as 1788 and, prior to the boom of the Industrial Revolution, they were also used by occupants carrying out cottage industries such as weaving. The terraces were mainly built in Leeds' industrial enclaves: Armley, Beeston, Harehills, Holbeck and Hunslet. Harehills Triangle is a pocket of terraces of particular interest today for academic studies, due to the wide-ranging ethnicity among its residents. Historically, this close-knit living had its advantages, as clubs were formed, including early building societies, and there was a certain comfort for parents to know their children were playing street games within calling distance.

The red and brown brick houses were under pressure in the mid part of the 20th century, as their advantages soon turned into negatives. Back-to-back living was viewed as unhealthy (many shared toilets) and culturally threatening, which led to a huge chunk of them being demolished. These days, a wide range of people from many social backgrounds rent or buy the remaining terraces, ensuring they are still very much part of Leeds' furniture.

Address Harehills Triangle can be found around Elford Road / Elford Place, LS8 5LE |
Getting there Bus 4, 12, 49, 50 or 50A to Elford Road; by car: take the A 64 and then
A 58 from the city, then Beckett Street and turn on to Elford Road | Hours Accessible
24 hours | Tip Nearby on Elford Place West, St Aidan's Church, constructed in 1894, is
built in an Italian Romanesque style and houses a huge 100-year-old mural, which is on
public display in the eastern apse.

5 — Barnbow Lasses Memorial

Gone but never forgotten

Their deaths were kept secret from the public for years, but this tribute to the heroism of the 'Barnbow Lasses' is a permanent reminder as well as a welcome solace for the many family members who make the journey to this corner of Leeds.

The memorial stone, which stands stoically in Manston Park, Cross Gates, is illustrated with iron carvings depicting the women dutifully carrying out their work at Barnbow, a shell factory that produced thousands of tonnes of ammunition during World War I. It is thoughtfully positioned, close to the site of the disused Barnbow, now designated a scheduled monument, and bears the names of the women and girls who died in an horrific explosion.

With most of Britain's men away fighting during World War I, it was left to the women and girls to keep the home fires burning and hundreds – some men included – were seconded to the Barnbow factory. Wages were high but conditions were poor. Women and girls worked lengthy shifts, seven days a week in their underwear in an attempt to fend off the searing heat from the hot water pipes. Most of the work required the 'Barnbow Lasses', as they were colloquially known, to pack the munitions with fuses. On 5 December, 1916, an explosion happened in Room 42 after incompatible fuses were packed. It resulted in the deaths of 35 girls – some as young as 14 – and left many more injured. The tragedy was hushed up and it was six years before the general public really knew what had happened that day, as the factory's existence was deemed top secret. Another five people also lost their lives at Barnbow in other explosions before the end of the war.

The memorial was unveiled in 2012 before a gathering of the victims' relatives, city councillors and the local archaeology group whose members campaigned for it to be made. The stone contains the words: *Their courage and sacrifice will not be forgotten.*

Address Manston Park, Penda's Way, Crossgates, LS15 8HS | **Getting there** Bus 40, 56, 64, 163 or 166 from York Street, city centre; by car: take the A 6120 / A 64 from the city centre towards Garforth | **Hours** Accessible 24 hours | **Tip** There are several streets and parks in Leeds named after many of the Barnbow Lasses. There is also a group of small stones bearing names of the victims at Crossgates near to the roundabout for the A 6120 Leeds Ring Road, and a Roll of Honour for them can be found inside Colton Methodist Church.

6 — The Barwick Maypole
You will have probably hummed its theme tune!

Many people in Britain will have hummed the theme tune to Radio Four's *The Archers*, but few know it was inspired by a lovely maypole that stands in the heart of Barwick-in-Elmet village. *'Barwick Green'*, the theme tune to the long-running rural drama, is subtitled 'A Maypole Dance', and was composed by Arthur Wood in 1924.

The maypole stands on the green in Barwick, which lies seven miles to the east of Leeds, and it is honoured every three years when villagers come out in force to celebrate the month of May. It has been a famous landmark locally for more than a century, despite being 'kidnapped' twice in a tug of love and war dispute involving rival villagers who claimed it originally belonged to them. Thankfully, the last attempt to snatch it – while it was taken down for cleaning – was 54 years ago. It was found abandoned on a nearby roadside, which has since led to a period of 'peace' between warring factions.

At 90 feet (27 metres) high and weighing over 1 ton, it is the tallest in Britain, attracting thousands to the tri-annual festivities. It is gingerly dismantled by volunteers before being elegantly preened and polished every three years in preparation for its big day. Each year, the celebrations come alive and the fun starts with a parade of the pole in the strong arms of the Barwick men and women who proudly carry it through the village before helping to hoist it into position. Then it is time for one lucky local to fulfil the dubious honour of shinning up to the summit of the pole (safety harnesses are provided) to turn the weather fox at the top, theoretically bringing good fortune to the village for another three years.

The British tradition of morris dancing takes place around the maypole with garlands and ribbons at the ready. A brass band accompanies, but no prizes will be awarded for guessing one of the tunes on the playlist!

Address The Cross, Barwick-in-Elmet, LS15 4JP | Getting there Bus 64 to Main Street; by car: take the A 64 out of Leeds towards York | Hours Accessible 24 hours | Tip The New Inn on Main Street, Barwick-in-Elmet, was once named Small Pub of the Year by the group Campaign for Real Ale (CAMRA). It is a lovely old pub with a real fire and great ales.

7 Battle of Adwalton Moor
A battle lost but a war won

Time has judged the Battle of Adwalton Moor to be one of the most significant turning points in the English Civil War, and it took place on high ground betwixt and between the West Leeds villages of Gildersome and Drighlington.

The fighting broke out on 30 June, 1643 and the site of the battle is marked on solitary ground with a plaque on stone and details of the conflict. The English Civil War was a hard-fought series of wars between the Parliamentarians (Roundheads) and the Royalists (Cavaliers). It was essentially a power struggle to democratise England and Wales by the Parliamentarians who were fiercely against laws and religions imposed solely by the monarchy. Soldiers from the Parliamentarians, headed by Lord Fairfax, were on the march to protect nearby Bradford but were overpowered by the Earl of Newcastle's Royalists at Adwalton Moor. The Royalists had twice as many soldiers as their opponents, and the luxury of canon fire. Around 500 of the Parliamentarians were killed at Adwalton with more than 1,500 injured. The defeat was a bitter blow for the Parliamentarians who were left with just one stronghold in Northern England: Hull. But it was the push needed for the Parliamentarians to join forces with the Scottish Covenanters in a political and religious alliance. Scotland had sympathised with the Parliamentarians' causes and so readily entered into the 'entente cordiale'.

One year after the Yorkshire battle, defeat turned into victory at Marston Moor near York and this was seen as the beginning of the end for Charles who went on to further defeat at Naseby, sealing the fate for the Cavaliers. Despite King Charles' execution in 1649, the war raged on for another two years until Charles ll was exiled and Parliamentarians, headed by Oliver Cromwell, took power. A re-enactment of Adwalton took place in June 1999 by members of The Sealed Knot.

Address Adwalton Moor, Adwalton, BD11 1DQ | Getting there Bus 254 or 255 to Drighlington Crossroads and a walk up to the moor takes around 10–15 minutes; by car: take the M 621 from the city then the A 650. The site is between the A 650 and the B 6135. | Hours Accessible 24 hours | Tip Stank Hall Barn, close to the White Rose Shopping Centre, is well worth a visit. Some of the timbers date back to the 1400s and were believed to be part of ships used by Christopher Columbus, but the main body goes back to the 1600s. It was reportedly used as a refuge by soldiers at the Battle of Adwalton Moor.

8 Beryl Burton Gardens

A sporting great in a league of her own

Sometimes ordinary people achieve extraordinary feats. The memory of one such achiever remains immortalised in a little corner of Morley, near Leeds.

The garden's entrance has a high iron arch that is engraved with the words *Beryl Burton Gardens*. When you initially enter you might notice a paucity of large visual gestures, such as dazzling flower beds or bronze statues. It is a quiet, unassuming and contemplative place, tucked away rather aptly behind the Yorkshire Bank off the bustling Queen's Street. It opened in 1998 as a posthumous dedication to one of its locals, Beryl Burton, OBE. She was a cycling phenomenon during the 1950s, 1960s and 1970s, both on the track and on the road. She was five times world champion over 3,000 metres, 13 times national champion and British All Round champion consecutively for 25 years. Not initially seen as a natural rider, Burton was encouraged by husband, Charlie – himself an amateur cyclist – to realise her potential.

Virtually unknown to folk outside Yorkshire during her heyday, Leeds-born Burton achieved all this at a time when women's cycling was known only as a 'Cinderella sport', meaning no huge wealth, pomp and Olympic ceremony or global adoration were waiting at the finish line. During her life, Burton was often spotted – albeit fleetingly – doggedly turning those wheels around the seven hills on which Morley is built.

To celebrate this vision, if you turn your head around to a back wall within the gardens, you will spot the showpiece of the place: a splendid wall mural painted by Tammy Hall. It depicts the curly haired Burton – head well down – riding her bike against the backdrop of a generic country road.

Blighted by ill health throughout her life, Burton died of heart failure in 1996 aged just 58. Despite these drawbacks, to many she forever remains the ultimate belle of the cycling ball.

Address Beryl Burton Gardens, 86A Queen Street, Morley, LS27 9BU, www.morley.gov.uk/beryl-burton-gardens | Getting there Bus 51 or 52 to Commercial Street, or bus 200 or 201 to Morley Town Hall; by train: two half-hourly trains to Huddersfield stop at Morley Railway Station and it is a 10–15-minute walk up the hill to the town centre | Hours Accessible 24 hours | Tip A statue of the late comedian, Ernie Wise, one half of Morecambe and Wise, can be found in Queen Street. Leeds-born Ernie – born Ernest Wiseman – won a local talent contest in Morley during his early years. The statue was unveiled by Ernie's widow, Doreen Wiseman, in 2010.

9 Both Arms

A parting gift from a Leeds lad

The writer, George Orwell, once said it was generally observed that 'painting and sculpture have never flourished in England as in France'. If he had travelled to Leeds in more modern times, he would have been duly forced to erase this inclusion from his essay *England, Your England*.

Yorkshire alone is rich in world-renowned artists and sculptors – Henry Moore, Barbara Hepworth and Damien Hirst, included – but often sadly missing from this illustrious list is Kenneth Armitage. His famous *Both Arms* sculpture stands in Nelson Mandela Gardens, which was officially opened by the late South African leader himself in 2001. The bronze sculpture with hands and arms outstretched, symbolises eternal offerings of non-discriminatory friendship to all – a fitting symbolism for the gardens in Millennium Square and a sentiment close to the heart of Armitage, whose work mainly featured images of truths and humanity. During the garden-opening ceremony, Nelson Mandela introduced himself as 'an unemployed pensioner with a criminal record'. The crowd promptly roared with laughter and forgave him for his earlier error when he mistakenly referred to Leeds as 'Liverpool'!

William (Kenneth) Armitage, CBE, was born in the Roundhay area of the city and studied at Leeds College of Art followed by the Slade School of Fine Art in London. During his time at the latter, he developed a love for marrying human forms with inanimate concepts into one expressive art form. He resumed his career after military service and was named 'Best International Sculptor' at the Venice Biennale during the 1950s. His love for the Yorkshire and Irish landscape (his mother hailed from Ireland), launched an equal competency in drawing and paintings. Armitage later established his charitable fellowships for young sculptors. *Both Arms* turned out to be his final parting gift to Leeds, as he passed away in 2002.

Address Calverley Street, Millennium Square, LS1 3DA | Getting there Bus 5, 27, 28, X 41 or 49 to Calverley Street and a 10-minute walk; from Leeds Railway Station a 10-minute walk via City Square, Park Row and Calverley Street | Hours Accessible 24 hours | Tip You can see more sculptures at the Henry Moore Institute next door to Leeds Art Gallery in the city centre. Moore was born 10 miles from Leeds in Castleford. An abstract sculptor, he is probably most famous for his reclining figures, one of which you can spy just outside the institute.

10 Braime Pressings
You may bump into a Peaky Blinder!

Viewers of BBC's *Peaky Blinders* and *World on Fire* may think this Grade II-listed Hunslet factory looks vaguely familiar – and they would be right. But when the cameras stop rolling, Braime Pressings goes back to its utilitarian self and it is business as usual.

Sean Bean's character met his daughter outside Braime in season one's war epic, *World on Fire*, as it doubled as the fictional Manchester factory, Tait and Somers. Cillian Murphy walked menacingly through a backdrop of welders' sparks and flames when it posed as a 1930s' car plant in an episode of *Peaky Blinders*. However, Braime's real claim to fame is that, in 1917, it was the first factory in Britain to open a canteen for its workers.

The Edwardian canteen still exists today, clothed in some of its original marble, oak and parquet features and – although no longer a place for the workers to eat – can be hired for weddings and other events. During World War I, Braime adapted to become a munitions factory and women made up around one-third of the workforce with the majority of men away fighting. Concerned for the well-being of the shift workers, the owners opened the canteen, which had separate floors for male and female staff.

Braime Pressings started life in a humble Hunslet workshop in 1888 when Thomas Braime made his first designs with a flypress. When Braime lost his thumb in an accident, he cleverly invented an industrial oil can that could be applied efficiently to machinery using a detachable spout and handle. The leak-proof oil cans proved a huge success and orders quickly multiplied. The emergence of cars on Britain's roads led to a sharp rise in demand for metal components, and Thomas invited engineer brother, Harry, on board to help him expand the firm. They moved into the 1914 brick terracotta building on Hunslet Road, which is still owned by the Braime family and is largely unchanged today.

Address Hunslet Road, LS10 1JZ, +44 (0)113 245 7491, www.braimepressings.com |
Getting there Bus 12, 13 or 13A to Leeds Dock; by car: take the A61 out of the city
towards Rothwell | Hours Consult the website for details on the hire of the canteen | Tip
The former Alf Cooke printworks across the road from Braime is also an interesting place
built in the 1890s. It is now Leeds City College, and open to the public on certain days of
the month, when tours take place.

11 Bramhope Railway Tunnel

Construction at a cost

Bramhope Railway Tunnel is a real bobby-dazzler of a structure, sporting a façade more in keeping with a castle than a hillside thoroughfare for passing locomotives. This early Victorian grandeur, designed by Thomas Grainger, was built between 1845 and 1849 on the Leeds/Harrogate/Thirsk line that runs through the Airedale and Wharfedale Valley. Its construction was ordered by landowner William Rhodes, of nearby Bramhope Hall, who allegedly wished to feast his eyes on a thing of beauty in the estate's rural landscape. There are two north and south Grade II-listed portals flanked by castellated turrets; the tunnel is just over 2 miles long and stands 25 feet (7.5 metres) high.

Construction was expected to cost around £800,000 but this figure was quickly leapfrogged with the final figure reaching around £2.1 million, a staggering amount in those days. However, no price could be placed on the human cost as, during its construction, up to 50 men were said to have lost their lives – twice as many as the official records suggest. A replica of the north portal stands in nearby Otley churchyard as a reminder of the sacrifices made. Work was highly dangerous for those who were employed to dig and blast the land, which was susceptible to subsidence and flooding. Life was generally tough as the tunnellers were forced to live with their families in basic shelters and fights often broke out among drunk and demoralised workers. A policeman was even employed to keep order, and a railway cart was frequently needed to take the injured to hospital, regardless of how they acquired their injuries.

The grand opening of Bramhope Railway Tunnel took place on 31 May, 1849, and the inaugural journey was made under the hillside by a George Stephenson-designed locomotive. Local residents opined that regular visits to the tunnel would also serve as fitting tributes to those who died.

Address Moorland Road, Bramhope, LS16 9HW | **Getting there** Bus X 84 from Leeds Merrion Street; by train: the tunnel can be viewed between Horsforth Railway Station and Arthington Viaduct on the Leeds / Horsforth / Harrogate line (you will need to walk from Otley Road and join a footpath to the railway cutting); by car: take the A 660 Otley Road into Bramhope village | **Hours** Accessible 24 hours, but take care near the railway lines | **Tip** Just opposite Bramhope Cemetery, you can visit one of the remaining Victorian lookout / sighting towers on Moorland Road, built to oversee the work. This was regularly used by James Bray, who was employed to supervise the tunnel's construction.

12   Bramley Baths
An Edwardian gem with a social conscience

This beautiful Edwardian public baths was in danger of going under 10 years ago before a group of die-hard stalwarts rescued it from oblivion, and lives have been saved as a result.

Built on the site of a foundry, this Grade II-listed building was opened as a public baths in 1904, but had seen better days until it was finally earmarked to go on the council's chopping block; that is, until a retiring MP fought its corner.

Bramley Baths is now a pearl of a place in the heart of a community whose voices are no longer ignored, thanks to a dedicated social enterprise team. The team was, and still is, headed by former Labour MP for Leeds West, John Battle. The rescuers raised some of their own capital as well as securing a grant from the Heritage Lottery Fund, and finally persuaded Leeds City Council to lease it permanently to them.

Today, Bramley Baths presents so much more than just a pool for the public: it is a thriving community hub with a communal garden and offers training in various skills including market gardening, sports coaching and accountancy. It is run by a 47-strong team of paid staff receiving more than the minimum wage. More importantly, it has, quite literally, thrown a lifeline to vulnerable members of society.

Reports of children drowning in the local canals due to a lack of swimming skills immediately prompted a campaign to encourage school teachers to take their children to Bramley Baths. Today, such tragedies are rare, thanks to the provision of regular lessons that are also offered to the over-80s, people with disabilities and learning difficulties as well as ex-offenders needing rehabilitation. Much of the baths has kept its Edwardian features with the original oak and stained-glass window ticket booth. The poolside changing cubicles, the Japanese steam room, gym, changing rooms and the dance studio, have all been sympathetically upgraded.

Address 414 Broad Lane, LS13 3DF, +44 (0)113 256 0949, www.bramleybaths.com | Getting there Bus 16 or 49 to Bramley Park | Hours Daily 7.30am–9pm but closing times may vary for the pool so check the website | Tip Bramley Community Centre nearby on Waterloo Lane, is also a thriving hub hosting local clubs, talks and exhibitions.

13___ Brick Man

Leeds' own Angel of the North

Was this the most missed opportunity in popular culture since Decca turned down the Beatles? Sir Antony Gormley's *Brick Man* sculpture could have been the original *Angel of the North*. However, Gateshead's gain was Leeds' loss.

Some consolation for art lovers is this considerably smaller life-size sculpture of Sir Antony's *Brick Man*, in a mummified form, which can be seen in Leeds Art Gallery. The original one was to be 98 feet (30 metres) high – almost half the height of Leeds' grand Victorian structural icon, the town hall.

In 1988, a then little-known Antony Gormley entered and won a competition to create a piece of superb public art for the centre of Leeds. To make the sculpture, he covered his own body in plaster to create his vision. His original idea was for the man to stand as a city beacon of light near the crisscross of the railway lines in Holbeck; a sign of a warm welcome and a fond farewell to those travelling in and out of the city.

Sir Antony wished that the original giant man would be a piece of art for everyone, accessible to explore, courtesy of hollow entrances and exits in the sculpture's heels and ears. The cost of the *Brick Man* would have been £600,000 but after garnering public opinion and a long look into an impecunious council money pot, plans were eventually scrapped. The then Labour-led Leeds City Council was headed by George Mudie, and was largely answerable to a Conservative government under Margaret Thatcher. After gathering opinion from both the public and his fellow politicians, he considered it too risky an investment.

Sir Antony – who went on to win the coveted Turner Prize in 1994 for his *Field for the British Isles* – was awarded a knighthood for his many subsequent pieces. After learning of Leeds' decision to abandon the project, a deeply disappointed Sir Antony was reported to have said that he believed the Council had simply lost its nerve.

Address Leeds Art Gallery, The Headrow, LS1 3AA, +44 (0)113 3785350 | Getting there Bus 14, 15, 19 or 19A to The Headrow; the gallery is also a 5-minute walk from Leeds Railway Station. | Hours Tue–Sat 10am–5pm, Sun 11am–3pm | Tip In the gallery you can also see *Hieroglyph*, a sculpture by Dame Barbara Hepworth, who was born in nearby Wakefield and studied at Leeds College of Art. There is a dedicated gallery showing Hepworth's work in Wakefield, approximately 9 miles from Leeds.

14 Brimham Rocks

Where a dancing bear meets a sphinx

Where would you find the Eagle with the Writing Desk, Donald Duck or General De Gaulle, and what connects them with three musical brothers from the Isle of Man?

The puzzle can be unravelled in a sculptural leftover of a natural erosion in the form of balancing rock formations. Brimham is a multitude of sandstone rocks – some 30 feet (9 metres) high – eroded by water, glaciers and wind, just a short car ride from Leeds. Experts have roughly put an age on them of 320 million years, and the eminent 18th-century archaeologist, Major Hayman Rooke, described them as 'a most wonderful assemblage'. Others have nicknamed them a 'mini Yosemite'. Brimham Rocks provides a perfect natural playground with its ravines, ledges and boulders, brought to life by the vibrant heathers and plants crouching in the rock's shadows. The rocks have been 'baptised' to include names such as The Sphinx, Dancing Bear … you get the picture by now; but they have also been used as a dramatic backdrop for television and film, such as the children's dramas *Roger and the Rotten Trolls* and *Knightmare*. They were teamed with a pair of dice and a black cat in a 1987 video of the Bee Gees' hit *You Win Again*, although how these are linked to the rocks is still a bit of a mystery.

Brimham is cared for by The National Trust these days, and there is now a shop, snack kiosk and a car park to accommodate the ever-increasing number of curious sightseers. The land has been designated a Site of Special Scientific Interest, and rangers tend to the wildlife and moorland, which includes species of rare heather and plants. Birds of prey are regular visitors to Brimham, such as the once endangered red kite, often seen scouring the crevices from the skies for hidden prey, along with rival buzzards. A note to Bee Gees *aficionados*: a panoramic view of the rocks is seen in the video, just over the two-minute mark.

Address North Moor Road, Summerbridge, HG3 4DW, +44 (0)1423 780 688, www.nationaltrust.org.uk | **Getting there** Bus 36 to Harrogate, then bus 24 to Pateley Bridge and get off at the Flying Dutchman at Summerbridge; it is then a walk taking the Hartwithe Bank Road; by car: take the Harrogate A 61, B 6165, B 6265 to Summerbridge | **Hours** Accessible 24 hours | **Tip** There are some lovely walks through the Nidderdale Valley from Brimham Rocks, such as those to Druids' Cave Farm, Pateley Bridge, Glasshouses Dam and Fell Beck, details of which can be found at the site.

15 Brudenell Social Club

Lammo's favourite

Broadcaster Steve Lamacq has described Brudenell Social Club as one of his favourite independent venues for live music in the country, and the compliment has been seconded by artists, critics and music lovers.

The serial award-winning venue, Brudenell, provides a platform for new bands to play to discerning music audiences, yet it has also attracted huge names such as The Charlatans, and Fleet Foxes. Regulars to the Brudenell have included Leeds-formed bands such as The Wedding Present, Alt-J, The Ukranians, Yard Act and Kaiser Chiefs. The latter played a secret gig at Brudenell in 2007 along with The Cribs and Franz Ferdinand. Brudenell Social Club was founded in 1913 by a group of local businessmen who built a wooden club house for working men in Queen's Road, Brudenell, a district named after the family who owned many of the local pubs in the area. Wear and tear over the years led to its replacement in 1978 by a firmer, brick building, and responsibility for the club was taken up by the Clark family in 1992, who started organising live gigs to accommodate the burgeoning local student population. In 2004, Brudenell's future was put in doubt following complaints from residents about the noise levels in this densely populated area. A series of fundraising activities took place to cover the cost of sound-proofing measures which, together with lottery cash, raised the money needed and sealed its long-term identity.

In 2007, Brudenell transitioned from a private, to a publicly owned club with Nathan Clark taking up the mantle from his parents. Today, Brudenell includes a gig space with a capacity for around 400 people, a games room, bar area and the Community Room, which opened in 2017. Staff are paid a living wage but all the profits are ploughed back into the cost of running the venue. The Wedding Present returned in 2013 to play a gig marking the club's centenary.

Address 33 Queen's Road, LS6 1NY, +44 (0)113 275 2411, www.brudenellsocialclub.co.uk |
Getting there Bus 56 to The Royal Park Pub; by train: take train to Horsforth / Harrogate
and get off at Burley Park Station | Hours Sun–Thu noon–11pm, Fri & Sat noon–mid-
night | Tip Belgrave Music Hall and Canteen at Cross Belgrave Street in the city centre, is
also a great place for live music, comedy and film.

16 The 'Burley Banksy' Electric Boxes

Symbols of hope for Leeds fans

Turn any corner when strolling near Elland Road and surprising pieces of street art await … on electric boxes! They are the work of a Leeds primary school teacher, Andy McVeigh, who has been dubbed the 'Burley Banksy' by fellow football fans.

Andy has been brightening up the streets around Leeds United's football ground, not only lifting spirits but raising awareness on mental health issues. More than 40 dull green electric boxes have been painted by Andy and more are planned. He has even crossed over the sporting divide and painted a tribute to two England cricketing heroes from the 2019 Ashes series. An electric box simply stating 'Stokes 135, Leach 1', makes sense to cricketing devotees. The boxes are now a symbol of good luck for the fans, with hundreds touching the artwork for good fortune on match days, and they have been widely praised for the precision of the artwork and their uplifting pictures and messages. Words such as 'We've been through it all together' are included in the portfolio, but there are several reverential nods to former players, and a special box dedicated to Gary Speed who took his own life in 2011.

Some of the artwork was erased with black paint in 2019 by a few anti-graffiti campaigners who misunderstood the artist's intentions. The disappearance of the paintings led to widespread outrage and Andy received public donations towards the cost of materials so that he could recreate them. Gary Speed's tribute was especially close to Andy's heart, as the tragic loss of a friend and his own niece, Grace, who died at just six months, led to a bout of depression that has been eased by his new – now commissioned – projects. The boxes around Kirkstall Lane depict Andy's other loves including music, nature and a touching tribute to his niece.

Address Elland Road, LS11 0ES, but the boxes are dotted around the Elland Road stadium, Beeston Hill and Kirkstall Road, LS4 2DN | Getting there Elland Road: bus 51, 52, 54 or 55; Kirkstall Lane: bus 33, 34, 35, 60 or 508; by car: follow the M 621 from Leeds centre and turn off at Elland Road Stadium | Hours Accessible 24 hours | Tip The back of the Peacock Pub across the road from the stadium transforms into The Spiced Mango Indian Restaurant on non-match days, offering delicious cuisine. On match days, the kitchen and restaurant close, giving way to the expansion of The Peacock, which takes over the entire premises.

17 __ Burton's Demob Suit

It really is 'The Full Monty'

The economic rise of Leeds in the early 20th century was largely due to the tailoring industry, once the domain of many Jewish refugees forced to seek a new life in this foreign land. Perhaps the most famous among these migrants was Montague Burton, whose empire went on to become the world's largest multiple tailors.

An authentic Demob Burton three-piece suit – made in the 1940s – can be found on permanent display at Armley Mills Museum, which is just one example from the hundreds of thousands made especially for the homecoming troops following World War II. Burton arrived in Leeds with no spoken English and little money in his pocket. He vowed he would 'clothe the nation' and be the first to produce the 'five guinea suit': he ticked both boxes. Armed with these fulfilled ambitions, Burton added the demobilisation civilian suit, which was fondly called 'The Full Monty'. During World War II, one-quarter of the troops were clothed in a Burton-made uniform, and around one-third wore the 'Demob'.

Burton was born Meshe David Osinsky in 1885, but was forced to flee his homeland, annexed Lithuania, as a result of the persecution of Jews by Tsarist Russian pogroms. Within three years of his arrival to Yorkshire in 1900, Burton owned five shops in Sheffield and a warehouse in Leeds – a remarkable achievement for an 18-year-old. An early ambition to make 'overcoats for working men' was quickly realised in 1903 and the booming Burton's production led to the opening of Leeds' Hudson Road factory in 1922, employing more than 10,000 workers in its heyday. England's World Cup winning football team of 1966 each sported a Burton suit. Following Burton's death in 1952, Jackson the Tailor became part of Burton's, adding Top Shop, Top Man, Dorothy Perkins and John Collier. Despite a later takeover by the Arcadia Group, Burton still remains unforgettable.

Address Canal Road, Armley Mills, LS12 2QF, +44 (0)113 378 3173,
www.museumsandgalleries.leeds.gov.uk/leeds-industrial-museum | Getting there Bus 15
from Leeds Railway Station to the museum, or 33, 34, 35, 60, 508 or 757 to Kirkstall Road;
by car: take the A65 towards Armley from the city centre | Hours Tue – Sat 10am – 5pm,
Sun 1 – 5pm | Tip An original Burton Five Guinea suit can be found on display at Leeds
City Museum at Millennium Square in the city centre.

18 Captain Oates' Stone

A tragic hero who made the ultimate sacrifice

Many hold the mistaken belief that it was polar explorer, Captain Robert Scott, who uttered the ill-fated last words: 'I am just going outside and may be some time.' In fact, these were reported to be the final words of Captain Lawrence Edward Grace Oates, whose achievements are duly acknowledged.

Captain Oates was part of the five-man team of explorers on the Terra Nova Expedition attempting to reach the South Pole in 1912. They were beaten to the Antarctic pinnacle 34 days earlier by a Norwegian party led by Roald Amundsen. Grief and fatigue stricken, the British explorers began the treacherous journey home through the frozen wastes, but perishing conditions ultimately led to tragedy. Four bodies – Scott, Bowers, Evans and Wilson – were later recovered, along with Scott's diary that recorded Oates' final words; Oates' body has never been found.

The commemorative stone is embedded on the gatepost of Holy Trinity Church close to Meanwood Park, which was largely owned by Oates' paternal grandfather. Although London-born, a young Lawrence spent much of his time in Leeds as both parents hailed from Meanwood. Oates was chosen to join Captain Scott's team due to his sublime knowledge of horses, which were vital four-legged additions to the expedition. He acquired equine expertise while serving as a soldier in the Boer War; this, and a willingness to contribute financially to the polar project, guaranteed his inclusion. Oates was often derided by Scott as a bit of a pessimist. However, Captain Scott's final gracious account in his diary included words of utter admiration for his comrade, as he believed Captain Oates had made the ultimate sacrifice because he assumed his physical injuries might slow the others down. Oates took off his shoes and walked away barefoot, due to his acute frostbite. The stone's inscription reads *A very gallant gentleman*.

LAWRENCE EDWARD GRACE OATES
OF MEANWOODSIDE IN THIS PARISH
1880 - 1912
CAPTAIN 6TH INNISKILLING DRAGOONS
SERVED WITH DISTINCTION IN THE SOUTH
AFRICAN WAR. IN 1912 HE REACHED
THE SOUTH POLE WITH CAPTAIN SCOTT
AND ON THE RETURN JOURNEY HOPING
TO SAVE HIS COMPANIONS WENT OUT
FROM THEM TO DIE. HIS BODY LIES LOST
IN THE ANTARCTIC SNOWS. HIS NAME IS
HERE BY HIS FELLOW VILLAGERS RECORDED.

A VERY GALLANT GENTLEMAN

Address Church Lane, Meanwood, LS6 4NP | Getting there Bus 51 to Church Lane or bus 52 to Stonegate Road and it is opposite the cemetery at the old entrance to the church; by car: take the A660 Otley Road from Leeds centre; Church Lane lies between this and the A6120 | Hours Accessible 24 hours | Tip Leeds Civic Trust unveiled a memorial cross and a blue plaque also in honour of Captain Oates in 2012. It can be found in Meanwood Park.

19___Chapel Allerton

Where retail meets therapy

There are small pleasures to be taken in the knowledge that even large cities have their cosy pockets where you are invited for a spot of retail therapy and a chat. They rub along just nicely thank you, away from the clutches of the chain stores.

Chapel Allerton remained a village until the 1900s, independent from Leeds, but even the blurred lines of urbanity cannot erase the genuine warmth of a small town in the country vibe.

The beating heart focuses mainly on Harrogate Road, Town Street, Regent Street and Stainbeck Corner, where you find the former police station and library on the triangular edge. Another cluster of heritage buildings can be found scattered in the nearby vicinity. Almost all the bright and welcoming little independent shops have a story to tell. Where else would you ask for a 'Cold Bath', short-back-and-sides special or enjoy a cup of tea in the company of Alley Cats? Alternatively, munch on Mexican tapas at Pinche Pinche, or bag a favourite Leeds invention like Spirograph and Cluedo at the well-stocked Armadillo Toys. Local boys, Sooty and Pudsey Bear said they were in a meeting that day.

The streets are teeming with businesses carrying the most pleasing of names, such as The Perfumed Garden Florist, Sunshine Bakery, The Cup and Saucer By Opposite, and Paria, a new café and cycling shop. Real thought has gone into making Chapel Allerton special, because it isn't just the bars, coffee shops and restaurants that cater for the customers' needs. It is filled with differing arts, crafts and well-being hubs. The Café Psychologique operates through Seven Arts space each month, offering not so much tea and sympathy but 'coffee and a chat'. Seven Arts on Harrogate Road is an organisation that runs film screenings, painting, live arts, dance, 'Kill for a Seat' comedy sessions and music on a drop-in basis. Psychologique recently ran an event entitled 'Failure: One thing I Know I'm Good At'!

Address 31A Harrogate Road, Chapel Allerton, LS7 3PD, +44 (0)113 262 6777, www.sevenleeds.co.uk | Getting there Bus 2 or 36 to anywhere on Harrogate Road / Regent Street | Hours The shops are mainly open Mon – Sat 9.30am – 5.30pm, but Sundays may vary depending on the type of shop; for Seven Arts it is advisable to check the website | Tip The Chapel Allerton Arts Festival has been held for the last 20 years and takes place over five days, usually on the last weekend in August. It is filled with live music and theatre, and many fringe events take place around the suburb.

20 Chippendale Collection
A master of all trades

In 2010, an exquisite piece of 18th-century furniture was sold at Sotheby's in London for more than £3 million. The Harrington Commode, a lavish dressing table, complete with pier mirrors, drawers and brass knobs on, was made by Otley's most famous son, Thomas Chippendale. His furniture and interior designs can be admired during a visit to the stately Harewood House.

Harewood was built in the 1760s for the Lascelles, whose descendants are still in residence. The house is pronounced 'Hairwood' by locals but 'Haarwood' by the not so down-to-earths. Chippendale – already known for his fine craftsmanship – was given the princely sum of £10,000 to furnish the grand home, and hardly a room was left untouched by the furniture maker's Midas magic. Such was his ranging talent, Chippendale even turned his hand to interior design and soft furnishings, which are still in evidence when you take a stroll through the gleaming rooms.

Thomas Chippendale was born in Otley in 1718, and it was his father, John, who played a pivotal role in his life, teaching his young son how to master his trade. He attended the former Prince Henry's Grammar School at Manor Square in Otley, and left Yorkshire in 1754 for London, where he established his worldwide status as the finest craftsman in his field, mostly creating pieces in mahogany, walnut and cherry. Chippendale, and William Kent before him, were known to have created 'a golden age of furniture' during the late 1700s.

Not all of the original furniture made at Harewood is on display, as a few exquisites have been donated to other museums and stately homes across the country, but there are plenty to be admired. Japanned night tables, wine coolers, pier glasses, pelmets and library chairs, beds, cabinets, intricately carved banisters – all invoke a sharp intake of breath for their beauty and leave one with a sense of awe for the master.

Address Harewood House, Sandy Gate, LS17 9LG, +44 (0)113 218 1010, www.harewood.org | **Getting there** Bus 36 to Sandy Gate; by car: take the A 61 Meanwood Road then A 61 Harrogate Road and follow the brown signs for Harewood House | **Hours** Daily 21 Mar–1 Nov, house 11am–4pm, gardens 11am–6pm | **Tip** You can visit a full-sized sculpture of Chippendale in his home town of Otley outside his old alma mater – now the Stew and Oyster pub – in Manor Square.

21 City Varieties Royal Box

A royal affair played out at City Varieties

They used to say that men in top hats would frequent Leeds Grand Theatre and those in flat caps used to take their pew at the City Varieties. Quite where the women got to was anyone's guess, but both theatres have survived, and the latter is now the oldest music hall in the country.

It was built in 1865 for Charles Thornton, above the Swann Inn, which still sits happily in its shadow today. One man in a top hat who opted for a bit of a 'downgrade' was Queen Victoria's son, Edward, Prince of Wales, who was a regular surreptitious visitor to the City Varieties. The Prince, who later became King Edward VII, would sit sheepishly, hunched over to watch his mistress Lillie Langtry, a married socialite actress whom the Prince met during a party one day in the 1870s. The affair began when a friend whispered in Lillie's ear that the Prince was 'interested in forming a friendship'. He was so enchanted, he would regularly risk being found out by watching her on stage. He used to travel incognito to Leeds and sit in the Royal Box, gingerly pulling the red velvet curtain to screen himself from men in flat caps. He would admiringly watch Lillie perform through a tiny gap in the drape. The affair came to an end in 1880, but Edward donated the Royal Crest to the theatre in gratitude to the discretion of the staff, and it still hangs in the auditorium today.

The role this small music hall played in the royal scandal intrigued many, and the acts that followed Lillie on the stage ranged from Houdini to a woman who hypnotised an alligator. It caught an early television producer's imagination as the theatre was chosen for recordings of *The Good Old Days*, from 1953 to 1983, which was allegedly watched in the royal household. Today, you are more likely to catch ex-Sex Pistol, John Lydon on the eclectic programme of shows and tours can be booked for a little nosey at the royal box.

Address Swan Street, LS1 6LW, +44 (0)113 243 0808, www.leedscityvarieties.co.uk |
Getting there Bus 7, 49, 50 or 50A to The Headrow; or a 10-minute walk from Leeds
Railway Station | Hours Check the website and box office for performance times and tours
of the theatre | Tip Just up the road on Millennium Square you will find The Carriageworks,
a new theatre complex housed in the former 1848 Stansfield Chambers and Electric Press
building. It has two theatres and six rehearsal rooms, and provides stages for local and
regional performers.

22 The Devil's Toenail

'If you build it, they will come'

The charming market town of Wetherby has long been associated with its fine racecourse, and was once named as 'one of the best places to live in Northern England'. A 1985 film starring Vanessa Redgrave, shot in the town, even bore the name in its title. Locals are rightly proud of this handsome place, which sits close to the receding borders of West Yorkshire.

One welcome addition to Wetherby opened in 2019, thanks to a group of resilient volunteers, eager to appease the interests of the young in the town. Hundreds gathered for the opening of the Devil's Toenail – a mountain bike trail park that has been radically transformed from a patch of wasteland in Wetherby, into a myriad of landscaped undulating paths, pump tracks and jump lines. The mission was achieved largely by members of Wetherby Bike Trails, standing side by side with SingletrAction, with the latter responsible for the maintenance of the Red Kite and Little Pump Trails, both of which are situated in the town. They dug their heels into spades to clear mounds of stone and mud, paving the way for the park. They even managed to persuade owners of the land to sell it to Wetherby Town Council for just £1 in order to kick-start the project. Lottery money – most of which came from Sport England to meet the £32,000 cost of the project – was gratefully received and, finally, they were off!

The trail is looped and graded and there is a section for basic riders, intermediates and a black, reserved for the expert riders. A jump line 'Flying Ginger' was named after James 'Ginger' Lacey, the famous, decorated World War II RAF fighter pilot, who was one of Wetherby's most famous sons. The trail also includes a picnic area, Watsons' Meadow, which was named after the family who owned and sold the land to the town council, and 'Mainline' which offers details on Wetherby's links with the age of steam.

Address Harland Way, next to Sustrans Route 67, LS22 6YR, www.wetherbybiketrails.co.uk | **Getting there** Bus 7 or X99 to Station Gardens, Linton Road stop and walk straight ahead to the cycle path; Devil's Toenail is adjacent | **Hours** Accessible 24 hours, but advisable to check the website in case of maintenance closures | **Tip** Sustrans Route 67, next to Devil's Toenail, is a national cycle route, situated on the former railway track, which runs from Leicestershire to Northallerton in North Yorkshire. The Chesterfield to Leeds stretch forms part of the famous TransPennine Trail.

23 __ The Domino Club

Minus the barbershop singers

The Domino Club is almost strangely reminiscent of 'Seb's' in the final scene from *La La Land*, where you might expect to see Ryan Gosling playing mournfully at a piano and wondering ... a spoiler will be resisted for anyone who hasn't yet seen the film. This basement speakeasy is a welcome addition to the nightlife chorus in Leeds.

Stepping into the Domino Club from the Grand Arcade is an intriguing affair, as you have to reach it through award-winning Lords' Barbering, an elegant voluntary hair loss business that advertises 'cut-throat razor' services: cue, flashback to a generic gangster movie. Thankfully, the violin cases do accommodate legitimate instruments and the barbering staff are very cheerful, helpfully cordoning off the shop after closing time to leave a chequered tiled pathway to the basement door.

Domino is essentially a jazz club, but its musical offerings are rich and varied on the neon-lit bijou stage, which comes to life Wednesday to Sunday. The basement was vacant under the arcade for many years, but the cobwebs were dusted and it is now the stylish club we see today. Blues, jazz, funk, reggae and soul are offered, courtesy of live acts such as The New Master-Sounds, who returned to their native Leeds following global success. The initial idea for the club was to give local bands a platform, and this notion still remains. But the word spread across the Atlantic, and Domino bookers were soon fielding calls from musicians in New Orleans and Los Angeles, eager to play at the club.

Music apart, a nominal fee is required before entry, and while you await the entertainment, bar snacks are on sale and cocktails are served at your table, courtesy of trained mixologists. Whisky and cognac are the speciality, but beers and wines are also on offer. The alcove leather seats and subtle lighting all add to the cosy ambience of the club. 'Nice'!

Address 7 Grand Arcade, LS1 6PG, +44 (0)113 318 2964, www.thedomino.co.uk | **Getting there** Bus 7 or 11 to the Grand Arcade, New Briggate | **Hours** Wed–Sun 6pm–3am | **Tip** Rolands, close by in Call Lane, is a little off-shoot club of The Domino, offering cocktails and a good ambience.

24 Dry Stone Walling
Perfect for beginners

An inspiring garden entitled 'Welcome to Yorkshire' scooped the coveted Gold Medal at the Royal Horticultural Society Chelsea Flower Show in 2018. One of the stunning centre pieces of the show-garden was a rural structure, synonymous with the county: an iconic dry stone wall. These distinctive walls can initially be spotted in some of Leeds' northern and western semi-rural suburbs, serving as a sort of starter before the ubiquitous main course begins. The ancient skill of dry stone walling can be acquired courtesy of lessons run by the Otley and Yorkshire Dales branch of the DSWA, a registered charity dedicated to keeping the art alive. Beginners' classes are arranged at weekends in spring and summer months where demonstrations and instructions are offered to folk from the ages of 13 to 80.

Historians have yet to establish how long dry stone walls have existed, but some are thought to go as far back as medieval and even Neolithic times. However, post 18th century-built walls can usually be identified, as they are fairly standardised, standing 4 feet (1.4 metres) high, and more often than not comprise a double row of stones topped with capstones, flat stones with a rounded top, often set vertically. As the name suggests, dry stone walls are so intricately assembled that they do not require such fillers as cement to hold them together; hence the instruction for their construction and the skill, which can take years to perfect. They are still a preferred farmland boundary marker in Yorkshire and materials are often sourced from nearby quarries or from recovered stones sporadically lying on the land. They are not just the domain of the county; they can be seen in many parts of rural Britain, although Yorkshire's lighter limestone walls give them their distinctive look. James Atkin, former lead singer with 1990s band EMF, is said to be a fan of the Otley course.

Address DSWA headquarters Arthington Garth, Arthington, Bramhope, Otley, LS21 1QD, +44 (0)1943 878 355, www.otleyyorksdalesdswg.org; exact locations can vary so check the website, and under-16s should be accompanied by an adult | **Getting there** For Otley town, bus 36 or X 84 from The Headrow, Woodhouse Lane and University of Leeds; by car: take the A 660 Otley Road from University of Leeds | **Hours** Daily 9am – 4pm, but check the website as these may vary | **Tip** Those who travel for the dry stone walling courses from afar might like to check out Otley Chevin Country Park Hotel, set in beautiful grounds with spa facilities and a gorgeous lake at the rear of the hotel.

25 Empire Palace Stone

Remnants of the golden age of theatre

The Leeds-born polymath, Alan Bennett, once observed there was scarcely a place in Britain to be found that didn't boast its own Matcham theatre. He was referring to Frank Matcham, a prolific architect in his time, whose legacy can still be found in the heart of the city.

Sadly, unlike many of Matcham-designed theatres still standing today, Leeds' Empire Palace Theatre had its last curtain call in 1961; a small but significant clue to its existence remains if you crane your neck skywards above the rear entrance of the Harvey Nichols store. The journey to view the stone is peppered with grandeur as the stunningly beautiful Victoria Quarter/County Arcade acts as a glorious gateway before turning into the lovely Cross Arcade where you will find the stone.

Matcham's Empire Palace Theatre in Briggate opened in 1898. It was part of an ambitious scheme by Leeds Estate Company to provide a theatre and dual arcade complex – Cross and County arcades – to stand alongside Thornton's Arcade, which opened in 1878.

The Empire Palace had a 1,700 capacity and contained cutting-edge features such as an electric light, sliding roof and a fire safety curtain. As well as live performances by huge names like Charlie Chaplin, George Robey and Harry Houdini, it was the first in the region to introduce talking pictures in the 1930s.

The Leeds theatre was also famous for staging one of Laurel and Hardy's final UK shows during their legendary tour in 1954, the inspiration for the 2019 film, *Stan and Ollie*. It also gave a platform to up-and-coming Leeds-born stars such as comic writer Barry Cryer, poet and playwright Tony Harrison, and the aforementioned Alan Bennett.

Rising television audiences led to dwindling numbers of theatre-goers and a die-hard core of protesters organised a sit-in to argue over its closure, but it was demolished in 1962 and the Empire Arcade built in its place.

Address County Arcade, LS1 6BE | **Getting there** Bus 1, 1A, 7, 7A, 7S or X7 to The Headrow | **Hours** Daily 10am–7pm | **Tip** If you cross over Briggate to 18–21 Lands Lane, you will find the Easy Hotel. Look up and you will see that the façade looks like an old theatre. That is because this was once the 1922 movie theatre, La Scala. At the back of the hotel there is still a remnant of the theatre: an old stairway that was the rear entrance to the theatre.

26 __ The Fenton

At the heart of post-punk

Leeds has always been an undersung city as far as popular music is concerned, often seen as 'an also-ran' in a race with Manchester and Liverpool. In fact, the city played a pivotal role in the post-punk movement during the early 1980s, trailblazing the way for a disaffected group of students and academics, with a desperate desire to shout above the noise.

The Fenton in Woodhouse Lane provided the perfect springboard for emerging post-punk bands, largely formed in local arts schools, the former polytechnic and the university, during the late 1970s and early 1980s. Gang of Four (GOF) and The Mekons were two such Leeds bands who were inspired by the energy of The Sex Pistols and wanted to keep the punk flames alive, while taking a left turn into a new wave era. The bands initially shared rehearsal space next to The Fenton, but needed more elbow room, which led to the offer of regular gigs in the pub. The early performances of The Mekons and GOF led to word spreading round the lecture rooms that The Fenton was THE place to be for other Leeds student bands, such as Scritti Politti and The Three Johns, the latter of which was formed by The Mekons' guitarist, Jon Langford. Two of The Mekons' bassists were female – groundbreaking at a time when roughly 50 per cent of the population were largely seen and not heard. Julz and Bethan went on to form Delta 5, because the counter culture at The Fenton fuelled a 'can-do' ethos.

Today, The Fenton looks much the same. Those who complain that the décor is a bit – well – basic, are missing the point. It was an important venue for radical thinking, and has refused to lose its heart and soul. A large chunk of customers are still students, and it remains a niche music venue for bands and stand-up comedy acts. Many former post-punk frequenters of the pub have since lamented there will never be another place quite like The Fenton.

Address 161–165 Woodhouse Lane, LS2 3ED, +44 (0)113 243 1382,
www.thefentonleeds.com | Getting there Bus 1, 25, 27 or 28 to Woodhouse Lane /
Fenton Street | Hours Mon–Wed noon–midnight, Thu noon–1am, Fri & Sat noon–2am,
Sun 3–11pm | Tip The Eldon, a short distance away from The Fenton on Woodhouse Lane, in
almost touching distance to the Mechanical Engineering building at University of Leeds, was
also a popular pub with students in the 1980s, something that has remained unchanged today.

27 _ Fulneck Moravian Settlement

A slice of Czech with links to The White House

Moravia lies in the eastern part of Czechia and during the 1700s was ruled by Habsburg emperors who were intent on Catholicising the country. The Moravians wanted to continue practising their beliefs in peace and carry out their missionary work, so many opted to flee their homeland. They built small enclaves in which to live and very few survive; however, one remains virtually unchanged, tucked away at Fulneck.

The Fulneck Moravian Settlement was built on high ground here, probably to make the most of the stunning views over the Tong Valley, which also remains virtually unspoiled. The Moravians, who were members of the Bohemian Unity of Brethren Church, built cottages, shops and a chapel – still used by a local congregation. Established in 1753 is the independent Fulneck School, which has around 350 pupils. Notable alumni include suffragist campaigner Elizabeth Wolstenholme, actor Dame Diana Rigg and former prime minister, Herbert Asquith. The settlement carries much of the authenticity of its era, with cobbled streets, and a flurry of stained-glass windows on handsome buildings with clock towers. The chapel, built in 1746, contains detailed original documents of families living here since the 1740s, and also includes a superb original Johannes Snetzler organ. The graveyard accommodates tombstones lying horizontally on the ground to mirror the ethos of equality among the Moravians.

Visitors can take a walk around the settlement, but the tiny museum, school and chapel can be viewed only by appointment. A former resident is Benjamin Latrobe, one of the architects of The White House in Washington DC, and Yorkshire and England cricketing hero Len Hutton, whose cottage stands near to the grand village gateway.

Address 38 Fulneck, Pudsey, LS28 8NT, +44 (0)113 256 4828, www.fulneck.org.uk |
Getting there Bus X14 or X15 to Pudsey; by car: take the A58 and B6154 Tong Road and
turn left into Fulneck | Hours Accessible 24 hours, but check the website for museum times,
which vary and are seasonal, and for a view inside the chapel | Tip If you walk through the
village, on the other side, standing looking down over a grassy bank, is Bankhouse Inn. On
fine days you can sit outside enjoying the views over Tong Valley.

28__Gipton Fire Station
Proof that good people are still out there

The old fire station at Gipton was once one of the busiest in Britain. Firefighters and rescuers were called to some of East Leeds' most socially deprived places on a regular basis from its opening in 1937. The station closed in 2015 after relocating to nearby Killingbeck but is now a superb hidden gem.

Its incarnation was largely due to the vision of Julia Preston, with financial backing from the late Jimmy Heselden, a multi-millionaire philanthropist from Gipton who gave much of his fortune away to good causes in Leeds. Julia, a housing project manager for the local charity, Gipsil, spotted the fire station was for sale and persuaded Leeds Community Foundation – which looks after Jimmy's legacy – to donate money needed for the purchase. The fire station was given a satisfying makeover following the handover, but some of the original features remain, such as the firefighters' iconic poles, old pumps, the floors complete with frenzied wheel marks of the fire appliances and the engine room, now housing a café, along with the trademark colour of red paint, daubed throughout.

Six charitable groups (Gipsil included) operate independently at the old station and stand shoulder to shoulder with each other, unanimously holding a shared mantra that 'everyone is welcome' to this special community hub. Leeds Cookery School runs courses, and most of the profits are handed over to Zest, a local initiative in collaboration with chef Jamie Oliver's Ministry of Food, which offers nutritional support to families on low incomes. Those living with disabilities, the elderly and young people in care facing potential homelessness, are also supported through the other various socially conscious minds at Gipton.

Photographs and memorabilia displayed throughout the station serve as regular reminders to the life-saving work of the firefighters who regularly reunite there for a catch-up.

Address Gipton Approach, LS9 6NL, +44 (0)113 213 6813,
www.theoldfirestationgipton.org.uk | Getting there Bus 7, 11, 40, 56, 166, 403, 840
or 843 to Osmondthorpe/York Road/Gipton Approach; by car: take the A 64 (M)
York Road from Leeds city centre and turn off at Gipton Approach | Hours Daily
8am–9.30pm | Tip Fire Heritage Days are held every summer at the Old Fire Station.
Vintage engines converge at Gipton from all over the North of England. There are many
competitions, stalls and events taking place. The dates vary from year to year so it is
advisable to check the website.

29 Gledhow Valley Allotments

Digging their own, for victory

Allotments still remain a quintessential quirk of the British, with images of elderly gentlemen in braces donning flat caps among the vegetable patch. These days, you are more likely to spot a graphic designer or a lawyer 'down the allotment', digging heel to heel with the grandee green-fingered types who often show them how it's done.

With more than 160 plot holders and a growing waiting list (pun unintentional), Gledhow Valley Allotments is one of the largest and oldest in the country, with a far reach from Brackenwood to Chapel Allerton. Folk have been digging here since World War I when demand soared as land was transformed into neat rows of vegetables to keep the home fires burning. Those lucky enough to have bagged a plot at Gledhow pay Leeds City Council a reasonable sum of less than £50 annually, to continue with their self-sufficient lifestyles. Allotment holders run their own website with delicious recipes, tips and vital snippets of current green news. You can even access advice on how to make Martin's 'secret flapjacks' or Val's 'rhubarb clafoutis', or even 'Rob's 'rhubarb and orange cake': a Yorkshire theme is clearly here.

Beekeeping is popular, as well as the down-to-earth business of growing carrots and potatoes, which are now joined by 'posh kids' like kale and rocket. Public-spirited gardeners are happy to talk to visitors about their 'little darlings', and stories may be exchanged over cups of tea and coffee if you ask nicely. They even run their own small market garden business by selling the fruits of their labour at the plots, and profits go towards an allotment fund. Competitions are held at Chapel Allerton Methodist Centre each spring, summer and autumn when the green-fingered comrades can be spotted jostling to find out who the supreme champion grower will be in the differing categories. Seriously hard work is required here.

Address Off Northbrook Street, Chapel Allerton, LS7 4QH, +44 (0)757 088 4016, www.caagaallotments.org.uk | Getting there Bus 2, 3A or 36 to the allotments on Gledhow Valley Road or Harrogate Road; by car: take the Harrogate Road (A 61) from the city centre through Chapel Allerton | Hours Accessible 24 hours, but ask permission to enter the allotments first | Tip Gledhow Valley Woods is just a short hop from the allotments. There you will find lovely walks through well-signposted pathways. The Friends of Gledhow Valley Woods are a group of volunteers who help protect and preserve these woods.

30 — The Grand Arcade

Giving the glamour pusses a run for their money

The Grand Arcade was so often overlooked in the beauty pageant of shopping malls and heartachingly cast aside for other more obvious glamour pusses in the city; but take the time to wander under the glass ceiling and small treats await.

Built in 1897, the Grade II-listed arcade was designed by Leeds-based architects, Smith and Tweedle, in Renaissance style. The shops were pushed aside to make way for a cinema and, later, a nightclub from the 1920s until 2013, but it has beautifully emerged once again and is home to an array of independently owned, start-up businesses.

Just Grand, a vintage tearoom, is a quirky little café under the ownership of a co-operative. It offers high teas and a cheeky Prosecco or two at themed tables such as Buddy Holly and Elvis. Caribbean, Seafood, and Gents Afternoon Tea options are recent additions to the menu. Photography geeks who wish to take a break from the digital world will love West Yorkshire Cameras. It hosts a treasure trove of strictly analogue film cameras, lenses and accessories. The owner is always looking to buy quality 35mm medium- and large- format equipment to add to their offerings. The star attraction of the arcade is perhaps the eccentric 1898 Potts clock above the arched Vicar Lane entrance. Unlike the Ivanhoe Clock (see ch. 42), this little gem is the creation not of William, but of Robert, James and Joseph Potts. Locals helped raise funds for its restoration after it fell silent for 20 years. Two knights standing by a castle keep strike quarter hours, and a little hourly strike commences when a procession of seemingly random figures including a Scotsman, an Indian, a Canadian and a British guardsman emerge for inspection from one wooden door, salute in their own unique style, and return through the other. A cockerel flaps its wings above to bring the show to an end.

Address Grand Arcade, 20 Merrion Street, LS1 6PG, +44 (0)113 275 8758, www.grandarcadeleeds.co.uk | Getting there Bus 2, 3, 3A, 7 or 7A to New Briggate, then the arcade is just beyond the Grand Theatre and Opera House | Hours The arcade is home to some restaurants and the jazz club, Domino, therefore into the early hours. Normal shopping hours are 9am–5/6pm for retail outlets. | Tip Just a short walk from The Grand Arcade at 72-74 North Street is Wen's Restaurant, serving 'authentic home-cooked Chinese cuisine.' It has been described as one of the best restaurants in the city.

31 Hall Tower Hill

Two ancient forts for the price of one

Historical landmarks can turn up in all manner of places, and Hall Tower Hill in the village of Barwick-in-Elmet, is a perfect example of an ancient find off the beaten track. It is the site of a 2,000-year-old Iron Age fort overlooking sweeping agricultural land, and was later occupied in the 12th century by a motte-and-bailey wooden hill fortress.

The Iron Age fort can be found on the summits of two hills: Wendel and Hall Tower, with the latter reaching 50 feet (15 metres) high. The top can be appreciated by modern stone steps that are kindly provided to get you to the peak for a closer look. Evidence of the remains of a large entrance can be viewed from the northern side at Wendel Hill, and you can see a ditch and rampart known as 'The Slip'. Ancient coins and other relics were once uncovered but it is now protected from archaeological digs by English Heritage. The fort was built on magnesium limestone, providing an excellent natural drainage for agricultural soil, and experts believe it was probably used to protect the land from thieves and vagabonds.

The motte-and-bailey fortress was built on the south side at Tower Hill and this was thought to have been owned by the de Lacys of Pontefract, who ordered a fortress to protect the Elmet district of their kingdom. Later, a pottery works most likely operated at the site during the 17th century. During World War II, the twin hills were used by the Royal Observatory Corps to identify and track enemy aircraft, and concrete remains are still visible at the summit of Hall Tower. Local historians have a photograph from the time, containing illustrations of types of German war planes. The whole earthworks can also be closely scrutinised from ground level, using a series of footpaths at 'The Boyle', which lies to the northern edge of Wendel Hill and is where the two hill sites were divided by the Normans.

Address Hall Tower Hill, Barwick-in-Elmet, LS15 4JS | Getting there Bus 64 or X 84 to Main Street / Chapel Lane; by car: take the York Road (A 64) and turn off at Barwick village | Hours Accessible 24 hours | Tip All Saints' Church on Aberford Road, Barwick, is a lovely Norman church with remnants from Anglo-Saxon times. Tours, including Hall Tower, are occasionally carried out by Barwick-in-Elmet Historical Society.

32 The Harrison Clock
Time and tide waited for one man

Flummoxed scientists were frantically trying to come up with a solution to an international crisis during the 1700s, after thousands of lives were lost at sea. This was largely due to mariners' inability to pinpoint east/west directions (longitude) on the oceans, which led to miscalculating tides and positions. North and south (latitude) could be roughly calculated by the Sun's place in the sky and the Polar Star by night, but accuracy and knowledge of longitude was essential. This could only be determined accurately by knowing the exact time after weeks at sea.

In 1714, an Act of Parliament was passed offering £20,000 to anyone who could come up with a solution to measure accurately longitude time on the oceans. Wakefield-born John Harrison – a carpenter – took up the challenge. Derided at the time for his delusionary ambition, Harrison proved them all wrong and successfully met the complex brief, aided by his brother, James, by producing a long case pendulum clock that accurately solved this maritime problem. The 18th-century clock – one of three still in existence – stands proudly at the entrance of Leeds City Museum. It is a superb masterpiece and proved to be 50 times more accurate than any other clock. Harrison had not only new-found respect, he was awarded the £20,000, making him a millionaire by today's standards.

The main factor for its efficiency was Harrison's use of a tropical hardwood, lignum vitae, to make the clock, which used its own natural lubricant so that it would never have to be oiled. Clocks made from any other wood led to inaccuracy because they needed to be frequently oiled.

Fans of *Only Fools and Horses* may remember a popular Christmas special of the comedy when Del Boy and Rodney finally became millionaires after selling a rare pocket watch engraved by Harrison. It is a great nod to the Yorkshireman, who would have laughed.

Address Leeds City Museum, Millennium Square, LS2 8BH, +44 (0)113 378 5001, www.museumsandgalleries.leeds.gov.uk | Getting there Bus 1A, 1B, X 84 or X 85 to Woodhouse Lane or bus 27 or 28 to Great George Street | Hours Tue–Fri 10am–5pm, Sat & Sun 11am–5pm | Tip A short walk from the museum, on Cookridge Street, you will find the handsome Nation of Shopkeepers. This 'go-to' hub is built around a courtyard and offers live music, art, comedy and food and drink.

33 — The Haunted Staircase

Where spooky tales have come to rest

The 500-year-old Jacobean House, Temple Newsam, was the domain of the wealthy Ingram family for more than 300 years. It is known as probably the most haunted place in Leeds, and perhaps the spookiest part of the house is the utilitarian stone staircase provided for the domestic staff. Piercing screams have been heard on the steps by visitors, and things have been known to go bump in the night – quite literally, on numerous occasions. Chilling winds out of nowhere have been felt, and whispering takes place well after the visiting school parties have left.

Popular opinion is that the screams that appear are those of Phoebe Gray, a nursemaid at the house who fell to her death after unwanted advances from a brutish lout, William Collinson, who manhandled the young girl after guzzling a few pints. Historians say the murky deed was dealt on the night of a party thrown by the Ingrams in 1704 for the Duke of Marlborough. Phoebe had fallen to her death, but Collinson tried to cover up his crime by dragging her corpse down the steps and discarding poor Phoebe in the nearby well. After discovering her body, Collinson was tried for murder and hanged.

Perhaps the most famous of the home's ghosts is 'The Blue Lady', often seen shrouded in the colour. More ghostly screams have been heard on the magnificent central sweeping staircase. Carpets have suddenly rippled, and some witnesses have heard laughter. The chilling shrieks are thought to belong to Mary Ingram, young daughter of Sir Arthur. Mary was travelling back home in her carriage one night during the late 1700s, when she was robbed by highwaymen who stole her pearl necklace, a sentimental gift from her grandfather. The 14-year-old was so devastated she was said to have died from a broken heart. Mary's portrait hangs in the Gothic Room at Temple Newsam, which is known as the Hampton Court of the north.

Address Temple Newsam Road, LS15 OAE, +44 (0)113 336 7461, www.museumsandgalleries.leeds.gov.uk/temple-newsam | **Getting there** Bus 19 or 19a to Colton Lane / Laurel Hill Lane; by car: take the York Road (A 64) from Leeds and turn off for Whitkirk and Colton, turn into Colton Lane / Laurel Hill Lane | **Hours** Tue – Sun 11am – 3pm (pre-booked visits and guided tours on the hour) | **Tip** The house grounds were landscaped by Capability Brown and are splendid for walks. In the grounds you will also find the Home Farm, which is a great place for children and is home to some of the rarest breeds in Europe.

34 Hazlewood Castle

Not to be confused with Leeds Castle!

Just before the limestone high ground seamlessly melts into the flat-land of the Vale of York, a medieval treat of great magnitude awaits: Hazlewood Castle.

This Grade I-listed castle is now a handsome hotel and spa, loyally living up to its palatial name, with a mixture of original medieval trappings and replicated features. Hazlewood's roots go back to 1086 when the Domesday Book detailed Sir Mauger le Vavasour living on this large estate, now occupying 77 acres of land. The manor house was built in 1283 and later fortified and crenellated in 1286, with a folly added during the 18th century. The Vavasours occupied Hazlewood for around 900 years until the last descendant hung up the castle key and nipped over to New Zealand to run a vineyard in 1908. The noble family reputedly played host to Mary Queen of Scots in 1569 and Lady Anne Vavasour was a loyal aide to Queen Elizabeth I. The castle chapel has been around since 1264, and the family conducted Roman Catholic worship here – even during Henry VIII's reign when the religion was outlawed. They often shielded Catholic priests, and a subterranean exit once ran underneath to Crossroads Farm nearby, providing an escape route for the monks from execution.

Hazlewood has withstood bloody battles over the years, such as the Battle of Towton in 1461, during the Wars of the Roses. After a period of private ownership, it became a maternity hospital from World War II until the 1970s, and the castle apparently inspired many a new mum to name their bundles of joy 'Hazel' or, alternatively, 'Hazle'.

The Carmelite Monks moved in when the women and infants moved out, before it opened as a hotel. A few more mature Hazels have been known to return as guests. A healthy hybrid group of ghosts are seen and heard from cries of babies, to ghostly robed monks, strolling earnestly around the grounds. Question: Did they pay their bill?

Address Paradise Lane, Hazlewood, LS24 9NJ, +44 (0)1937 535 353, www.hazlewood-castle.co.uk | **Getting there** Coastline Bus from Leeds Bus Station takes you to the bottom of Paradise Lane, but the walk is around a mile-and-a-half; by car: J44 on A1 (M) towards York A64, then A659 and the Sherburn turn off, A162, before joining the A64 again on the opposite carriageway, then follow the brown signs | **Hours** Unrestricted for guests, but for spa and other activities, check the website | **Tip** Nearby is the charming village of Aberford, which was the crossing for the Great North Road. Aberford House is believed to stand on the site of a Roman fort.

35 Hetchell Crags
Yorkshire grit will take you to the top

Stunning landscapes are for ever knocking at the urban door of Leeds, waiting patiently in the wings ready to receive those city dwellers, secretly in love with the great outdoors.

Hetchell Crags offers a bit of Yorkshire grit in the triangular splendour of Bardsey, Thorner and Scarcroft villages, and can be appreciated from the safety of the firm ground during countryside walks. Geologists describe the crags as 'Upper Carboniferous East Carlton Grit' containing Namurian Millstone Grit for the pedants among you, but they are a delightful 30-foot (9-metre) -high little surprise in the pleasant countryside. Hetchell Crags' close proximity to sites of ancient quarries could have resulted in these being 'man-built', but formal evidence has yet to be submitted. Adventurous types can accept them for what they are and marvel at them, up close and personal with the aid of ropes, locking carabiners and boulder mats, and it is a safe-enough climb for beginners with the absence of overworked slippery rocks.

The crags form a perfect backdrop for the nearby Hetchell Woods Nature Reserve, just a foot slog away, and the climbing and scrambling zones are catalogued and given intriguing names. Walls and buttresses are bestowed with lists of themed titles. The Romanesque nooks and crannies are probably inspired by nearby Pompocali earthworks and include: 'Up Pompeii', 'Roman Crack', 'Tiberius' and 'Centurion'. Other walls include: 'Bell End', a ubiquitous name bandied about by the presenters of the BBC series *Top Gear*. Or could it be that it simply resembles a bell? The alarmingly named 'Dead Angst' awaits, along with the intriguing title 'Tear Across the Dotted Line'. Well-chalked hands will assist you to the slippery crevices of 'Grease' and 'Newton John'. Reaching the top will reward you with lovely views over the Yorkshire millstone grit-peppered countryside.

Address Hetchell Crags, Hetchell Woods, LS23 6NA | **Getting there** Bus X98 to Wetherby Road/Wood Lane and head to Hetchell View before following directions below; or those wishing a longer walk, bus 7 to Thorner village/Bramham Road; by car: take the A58 road to Bardsey and just south of the village there is a layby where you can park; or park at the Pompocali earthworks on Milner Lane/Home Farm Road, Thorner and follow the marked footpaths | **Hours** Accessible 24 hours | **Tip** Nearby Bramham Park Estate, Wetherby, provides a lovely day out with its grand 18th-century house and gardens, and is owned by the Lane-Fox family. The Leeds Festival takes place there each August bank holiday weekend.

36 Holbeck Cemetery
Watching over Leeds from Beeston Hill

Far from being haunting places of morbidity, some cemeteries can be enclaves of beauty, where stone inscriptions bear evidence of lives well lived. Holbeck Cemetery falls neatly into this category, with its grand entrance gates and looped paths, all landscaped and designed by Joshua Major, to guide bookworms unwilling to lift their head from the page as they strolled through. It opened in 1857, and stands imposingly on part of a former coal mine, watching over Leeds from Beeston Hill.

It hasn't always looked as handsome as it does today. Volunteers from the Friends of Holbeck Cemetery (FoHC) rallied together to rescue it from vandalism, once an incessant plague in the area, and made it into a garden of respect. Poet and playwright Tony Harrison's parents are buried in Holbeck Cemetery, and once on a visit he discovered to his disgust the cemetery was badly damaged. Such was his fury, he wrote the expletive-filled, poem 'V' in 1985, about an imaginary conversation with a drunken skinhead.

These days, Harrison will discover manicured lawns, flower beds and the ornate iron gates designed by Glyn Symonds. The gates – paid for by FoHC – display a series of picture clues depicting the professions of some of those buried in Holbeck, which include miners, railway workers, tailors, chemists and doctors. Grand tombstones cut a dramatic shape on the horizon, but some of the older graves belong to paupers and have no headstones; perhaps another motivation to write 'V'. There is a specially designated area for the 'guinea' graves, when the usual fee for a plot was waived and the poor were permitted to pay a manageable old English sum of one guinea.

Eve Tidswell, a member of FoHC, organises free tours and is clearly proud of this sacrosanct garden of peace, which is often a little disrupted by film crews. Scenes from *The Duke*, starring Helen Mirren, were shot at the cemetery in 2020.

Address Holbeck Cemetery Lodge, Fairfax Road, LS11 8SY, +44 (0)113 267 3188, www.holbeckcemetery.wordpress.com | Getting there Bus 10, 75 or 86 to Fairfax Road | Hours Accessible 24 hours | Tip Just around the corner on the right of Cemetery Road, you will find the childhood home of Ivy Benson (1913–1993). Ivy, a trailblazer for women musicians, was the first woman to lead the first all-female swing band. She and her band rose to worldwide fame during the 1940s.

37 __ Holbeck Working Men's Club

The oldest in Britain

Back in 1877, the first test match between England and Australia began, St John Ambulance was formed and one of the first gender equality speeches was given in London by American suffragist Victoria Woodhull. While these were all taking place, Holbeck Working Men's Club opened. This was not so much an historic event at the time, but it was a bit of history in the making, as today it is the oldest surviving WMC in the UK.

The club is, in fact, even older, for it was first established in 1871, at Ebenezer Place in Holbeck, but moved in 1877 to its present site – the former Low Moorside, now known as Jenkinson Lawn. By 1913 it had 426 members, but this figure soared to 718 in 1928. By the 1950s, the club voted in favour of allowing 'lady members' to join, a progressive and bold move for the time.

These days customers are more likely to spot a student serving behind the bar than a club member. Membership fees have been abolished, and the club operates on a not-for-profit basis, with the takings ploughed back into the general running costs kitty. Far from being stuck in the 19th century, Holbeck Working Men's Club has moved with modern times and Vice-President Dennis Kitchen, along with a small group of never-say-die members, fought tooth and nail to keep it open, despite the club teetering on the brink of closure in 2013. Changing habits, the smoking ban and rising alcohol prices had left it vulnerable. However, members turned things around, thanks in large part to a partnership with nearby Slung Low theatre company (see ch. 91), which previously shared premises with the club before moving up the road. However, there are still lots of activities going on at the club, including stretching and toning classes, lunch clubs and craft sessions.

Address The Holbeck, Jenkinson Lawn, Holbeck, LS11 9QX, +44 (0)113 226 0808, www.holbeckwmc.co.uk | **Getting there** Bus 54, 65 or 75 to Top Moor Side | **Hours** Mon, Wed, Fri, Sat & Sun 7–11pm, also Sun midday–4pm; open to members only, but membership is easy to obtain | **Tip** A short walk away on 17 Marshall Street, Holbeck, is a former flax mill, the Grade-I listed Temple Works. It was designed by James Combe in 1836 in the form of a beautiful Egyptian temple. At the time of researching the book, renovation works were being carried out.

38 The Horned Helmet
A gift from an emperor to a king

As gifts from Roman emperors go, the Horned Helmet is a rather eccentric one, but special nonetheless, and it is displayed for public delectation at the Royal Armouries Museum.

Affectionately known as 'Max', it was made by an Austrian, Konrad Seusenhofer, and presented to a young King Henry VIII by Emperor Maximilian I in 1514. Its main purpose was to be worn at royal court pageants and it was probably part of a full suit of armour, now lost.

Apocryphal tales have circulated that the emperor wanted the iron Horned Helmet to be a sort of cartoon version of the king, but it was initially mistaken for a court jester's hat with its brass spectacles, large pointy nose and spiralling rams' horns. One authentic regal likeness, though, includes a faint sign of stubble on the chin. Jokes about court jesters aside, the helmet was made with the king's comfort in mind, as it has generous holes for the eyes and mouth and a visor that lifts easily, together with a neatly finished base for an easy turn of the royal neck. After the death of Henry in 1547, the helmet was in danger of being lost for good when it was sold for scrap by Charles I. However, it was bought and rescued by a goldsmith and later restored.

'Max' migrated to Leeds when the Royal Armouries opened at Leeds Dock in 1996 as a solution to the bulging collection at the Tower of London. The vast collection of arms and armoury at the Tower led to a rethink about the location of a new museum away from London due to mounting criticism that cultural attractions were too 'Londoncentric'.

'Max' is encased on the second floor of the Armouries, which has free entry to everyone. The museum houses a large array of collections in themed rooms, including oriental, hunting, medieval and ancient war area. Throughout the year, the museum holds lectures and re-enactments including outdoor jousting events in the spring and summer.

Address Armouries Drive, Leeds Dock, LS10 1LT, +44 (0)113 220 1999, www.royalarmouries.org | Getting there 1-minute walk from Leeds Bus Station, 15-minute walk from Leeds Railway Station or a 12-minute ride in the little yellow water taxis from the railway station | Hours Daily 10am–5pm | Tip A short walk from Leeds Dock on the South Bank tow path will lead you to Leeds Climate Innovation District, a green corridor with lovely walkways and bridges built with reclaimed materials, low carbon homes and rejuvenated mills.

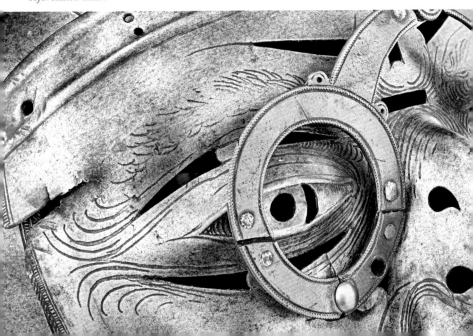

39   Hyde Park Book Club

But not just for literary types

Hyde Park Book Club is one of those cheerful places that holds a metaphorical mirror to Leeds' ever-changing image as a lively outgoing and culturally relevant city.

It occupies a former petrol station in the lively Hyde Park Corner and can safely be described as a place to chill out, listen to music, eat, read books, do a bit of online work if pushed, or contemplate life's twists and turns with friends over a glass of wine. The idea to create a place to simply 'hang out' and see what follows, belonged to socially conscious co-founders, Jack Simpson and Chris Walton, who had more anthropological reasons to open the book club doors other than simply making a fast buck. They run this social enterprise on an 'open door' policy for those who may be priced out of many of the city social hubs, and the chaps declared it wasn't for them to question anyone wishing to sit for an hour having drunk just a milky coffee. For the ravenous, wanting a bit of nosh, a sumptuous vegetarian menu is on offer, and the produce is sourced from the famous Dutch-based 'Vegetarian Butcher', aka Jaap Korteweg, whose plant-based foods have already won over swathes of fans. Grow Café provides the more locally cultivated greens. If it's 'Beans on Toast', you are after, *he* can be found on the entertainment menu in the basement, as he is a cult songwriter and folk singer who is just one of a huge eclectic queue of talented artists to have played on the tiny but impactful stage.

Hyde Park Book Club is also dedicated to championing classical and contemporary writers from Yorkshire and stocks a small, but carefully chosen array of books. Those working from home who could do with a bit of company are provided with space at the book club and it was here that Alex Sobel ran a successful campaign in 2017 to become Labour Co-operative MP for Leeds North West. Sir Keir Starmer dropped in one day too.

Address 27–29 Headingley Lane, Headingley, LS6 1BL, +44 (0)7984 449 361, www.hydeparkbookclub.co.uk | Getting there Bus 1, 1A, 1B, or X 84 to Headingley Lane | Hours Daily 10am–midnight | Tip Just up the road at Woodhouse Moor is the former Leeds Grammar School. It is a fine structure, built in 1859, but did you know this was where Richard Boon first met school friend, Howard Trafford. Howard renamed himself Howard Devoto and joined a band managed by Richard. They were of course, the Buzzcocks!

40 — Hyde Park Picture House

Voted the 'cosiest cinema' in Leeds

The long-awaited reopening of this magnificent Leeds gem took place in June 2023 after a £4 million, three-year renovation.

Hyde Park Picture House first opened in 1914, and such was the volume of complaints about men groping women in the dark, the owners installed nine gas lamps in the auditorium to deter the loathsome predators. Ladies' hatpins were backup safety precautions too, and during the refurbishment, many were recovered, along with original posters, programmes and Lyons ice-cream tubs from the 1930s. Some of these artefacts and newspapers from the Edwardian era are proudly on display now. Hyde Park Picture House remains the only surviving gas-lit cinema in the world, and it is a favourite with discerning film critics, such as Mark Kermode, who called it 'a lovely, lovely place.'

The much-needed restoration was possible thanks to National Lottery, and the City Council, and local film fans contributed as well. It includes soundproofing, a new extension and façade and a second screen on the basement level.

The picture house was built by Thomas Winn and was originally intended to be a hotel but when permission fell through, it was cinema's gain. The first film to be shown here was: Their Only Son (1914). The opening was timely, as it also screened World War I news reels. The original Edwardian ticket kiosk still takes pride of place in the foyer, although it is for historical reference only. Despite the nips and tucks, the picture house maintains its cosy atmosphere, with its ornately decorated upper balcony and stained-glass window in the foyer. The original terrazzo flooring uncovered during the works and has been restored.

But camera geeks and history buffs will be most excited about the two Cinemeccanica projectors that occasionally come out of storage to treat audiences to a cinematic magnum opus. Oppenheimer was on the wish list.

Address 73 Brudenell Road, LS6 1JD, +44 (0)113 275 2045, www.hydeparkpicturehouse.co.uk | Getting there Bus 6, 49 or 56 to Brudenell Road; by car, drive 8 minutes from the city centre down The Headrow onto Park Lane, then Belle Vue Road, Burley Street and Cardigan Road | Hours See website for schedule | Tip Quite close by at Cottage Road, Headingley is Cottage Road Cinema, another Leeds gem that is the oldest in the city, built in 1905 in a stable block. Cottage Road Cinema is now the only single-screen cinema in Leeds.

41__Inkwell Arts

A place of calm, creativity and clarity

Inkwell Arts is a huge bubble of fun, energy and ideas, throwing a much-need lifeline to those struggling with their mental well-being. One volunteer described it as 'a place which gives lots of clarity, through creative output'.

Inkwell opened its doors in 2009 after a few tweaks and brush strokes were carried out to the former Shoulder of Mutton pub in Potternewton Lane. It is run on a charitable basis with the support of Leeds Mind, and any profits made are ploughed back into the project. It is estimated that one in four people will experience some degree of poor mental health in their lives, but the stigma attached to the illness has diminished somewhat due to high-profile campaigns aimed at tackling the problem.

Inkwell is open to everyone over the age of 16, whether they live with the illness or not, but a few classes are offered for referrals on the advice of mental health experts. It offers a huge montage of activities, including workshops, talks and performances. Tutoring taking place includes African drumming lessons, art classes, sewing, acoustic nights, meditation, mindfulness and readers' groups. Intrigue occurs on the last Friday of every month, when a 'secret cinema' takes place and clues are given through social media as to the film's identity, but it is only truly revealed when the audience take their seats.

The café adds a new dynamism to Inkwell, and all the dishes cater for vegetarians and vegans, with local hand-picked food. Ingredients used are carefully chosen to decrease stress, and café customers can learn about diet and its correlations with mental well-being on a type of 'learn as you eat' basis. Exhibits of artworks carried out are proudly displayed at Inkwell and other public spaces in the city, and once a month the children can get their hands messy at Inkwell's Art Monsters sessions aimed at keeping the little ones happy.

Address 31 Potternewton Lane, Chapel Allerton, LS7 3LW, +44 (0)113 307 0108, www.inkwellarts.org.uk | **Getting there** Bus 2, 3, 3A or 36 to Chapel Allerton Hospital | **Hours** Tue – Fri 11am – 2pm, Sat 10am – 4pm | **Tip** Just a short walk away on Chapeltown Road is the stunning Sikh Temple Gurdwara. It is the largest temple in the area and is lavishly topped off with golden domes.

42 The Ivanhoe Clock

Robin Hood with bells on!

William Potts is probably as synonymous with Leeds as the names of Marks, Spencer and Burton. His trademark clocks can be spotted all over Britain's towns and cities. One splendid piece, with an added dash of Appleyard humour, is the Ivanhoe Clock in Thornton's Arcade. It's another little unique city gem, if you care to look up and see.

The clock contains life-sized wooden jacquemart (mechanised) figures from Sir Walter Scott's 1819 novel *Ivanhoe*, and nestles in the northern gateway in the impressive 1878 Thornton's Arcade. The clock chimes every 15 minutes, courtesy of Robin Hood and Gurth the Swineherd, and then it is the turn of Richard the Lionheart and Friar Tuck to strike the hourly bell. These merry figures were the design of Leeds-born sculptor, John Wormald Appleyard, a doyen in the field of stone masonry and carving. Appleyard's speciality was decorative and unusual figures, and William Potts was the clockmaker chosen to realise the design.

Potts established his Leeds business initially in Pudsey, before moving to the city's Guildford Street, in 1862. His reputation grew, and the firm was awarded a Royal Warrant in 1879 by Queen Victoria. Potts was joined by his three sons in the early 1900s, and between them they produced hundreds of clocks carrying the reputable name *W. Potts & Sons: Leeds*, although Ivanhoe's face remains plain. They were keeping time on buildings across the country's railway stations, town halls, pier heads and many other public landmarks. Leeds Town Hall and the Corn Exchange are just two grand Victorian buildings bearing Potts clocks that were soon in high demand globally – from Shetland to New Zealand. Potts is now a subsidiary company of Smiths of Derby, but the eponymous name remains. A book was published in 2006, detailing five generations of the clockmakers. Oh, and the author's name? M. S. Potts!

Address Thornton's Arcade, 30 Lands Lane, LS1 6LB, +44 (0)113 234 0184 | Getting there From Leeds Bus and Railway Stations a 5–10-minute walk via Boar Lane and Briggate | Hours Mon–Sat 9am–6pm | Tip Another interesting clock is the Dyson on The Time Ball Buildings, Lower Briggate, which carries an Appleyard design of the figure of Old Father Time with the Latin words *Tempus Fugit* (Time Flies). The building on which it stands was the former Dyson Jewellers' store in Leeds.

43__Jumbo Records
Still rocking in the digital age

A teenager walks into a record shop in Liverpool and asks a young Brian Epstein for a recording of 'My Bonnie' by a little-known group called the Beatles. Most of us know how the rest of the story pans out, but it was a pivotal moment like this that makes a vinyl store that most special of places.

Jumbo Records is the longest player in a rich list of record stores in Leeds, and has frequently been named by music buffs as one of the best independent vinyl shops in Britain. The first disc was spun in 1971 when DJ, Hunter Smith, opened the small but perfectly formed shop in the Merrion Centre before moving to a tiny balcony shop in Queen's Arcade, with an initial hardcore collection of soul and reggae.

Recent retiree Trevor Senior was a young man when he walked into Jumbo Records one day in 1973 and bagged himself a job. He was the go-to person for recommendations on all things Northern Soul. Jumbo Records was one of the first stores to play Marvin Gaye's *What's Going On*, and Trevor remembers listening to it for the first time at the shop as a fresh-faced customer in 1971. In those early days, cash-strapped customers often asked if they could listen to a snippet of their favourite song because they couldn't afford to enjoy the entire track; staff duly obliged. As glam rock gave way to punk in the 1970s, Jumbo moved with the times, extending the choice on offer and opting for bigger premises. It now stands firmly in The Merrion Centre, with an extended family of staff. Cody Barton is manager now, but Hunter and wife Lornette handed over the mixing desk in 2014 to Nick Fraser and partner, Justinia.

Jumbo is more than just a record store; it promotes small music venues, sells CDs, merchandise, concert tickets, books and magazines and has a small performing stage showcasing unknown bands.

Address 1–3 The Merrion Centre, Merrion Way, LS2 8NG, +44 (0)113 245 5570, www.jumborecords.co.uk | Getting there Bus 51 or 52 to Wade Lane and a 10-minute walk; on foot, a 15-minute walk from Leeds Bus Station and Leeds Railway Station via The Headrow, then turn into Woodhouse Lane, then Merrion Way | Hours Mon–Thu 9.30am–5.30pm, Fri & Sat 9am–5.30pm, Sun 11am–5pm | Tip There are some great record shops in Leeds, but Crash Records at 35 The Headrow is also well established after more than 30 years of trading in the city. It is also a go-to store for indie, punk, rock and metal, and stocks records by local talent.

44 — Kippax Bats

Fit for an England captain

What links a tiny corner of a village near Leeds, to some of the world's best cricketers?

The answer can be revealed in this small, family-run business in Methley, where you will find the staff beavering away creating the famous Kippax bat. It's a huge favourite with first-class cricketers such as former England captain, Joe Root. Root and his fellow England and Yorkshire team-mate, Jonny Bairstow, are regular visitors to Kippax Willow Ltd and have happily donated signed team shirts, which are displayed on the factory's entrance walls. Visitors can not only buy the bats if they so wish, but – by appointment – they can even witness the masters at work. Demonstrations are readily available on the craft of bat making; from the wood pile of the willow tree to the match-ready bat.

James is one of a tiny band of highly skilled bat makers you will find at the Methley factory and he will happily discuss sanders, cutters, pressing, pineapple blades and binders with curious onlookers as he places the semi-finished article in the 'oven-ready' climate room. The bats are all custom hand-made to suit the height and technique of the player, and the smoothness of the willow's grain is a key ingredient of the Kippax bat. The wood is sourced from purposely planted English willows near to the factory. Orders fly in from domestic and worldwide clients and some even make a special pilgrimage to pick up their bats in person from far-flung corners of the globe.

Kippax Bats was founded by the late Peter Kippax, a Huddersfield-born first-class batsman and leg spin bowler, who played for Yorkshire, Durham and the MCC in his time. Shortly after retiring from the game in 1987, Peter founded Kippax Bats, and the company has been running for more than 30 years. Son, Chris, has remained at the Kippax crease since taking over from his father, who died in 2017 at the age of 76.

Address Methley Lane, Methley, LS26 9HA, +44 (0)1977 550 303, www.kippaxcricket.co.uk | **Getting there** Bus 189 to Wakefield via Castleford to just after Methley Park Hospital; by car: turn left at Rothwell Sports Centre towards Castleford on the A639 | **Hours** Mon–Fri 9am–noon & 1–4pm, Sat 9.30am–noon but it is advisable to call beforehand for a demonstration or, alternatively, check the website | **Tip** Nearby, in the village of Oulton, at Rothwell Lane, is the 18th-century Oulton Hall, once the residence of the Blayds-Calverley family. It is a stunning hotel and golf course where non-residents can enjoy a lovely afternoon tea in the drawing room.

45 Kirkgate Market Domes

A piece of Victorian splendour

It is the scourge of modern times that many of us are far too busy texting or chatting to fully appreciate the splendour of Victorian architecture. However, the rewards are great if a little time is taken to marvel at Kirkgate Market's ornate domes.

The domes provided the *pièce de résistance* at the Vicar Lane section of the market when they were constructed in 1876 to showcase Leeds' wealth, paving the way for city status courtesy of a Royal Charter, in 1893. The architectural style is reminiscent of parts of Leeds' twin French city: Lille. Indeed, Yorkshire-born architects, Joseph and John Leeming, along with Richard Farrar, deliberately designed the domes with a Flemish style in mind. They are accompanied by 11 bays, chimneys and balustrades, all finished in granite, slate and lead casing, topped with a glass-domed ceiling. Many of the columns are topped by Atlantes figures, which were prominent features in ancient Roman architecture.

The domes were also lavishly built to house the market hall built later in 1904 which, in turn, complemented the popular open-air market, opened in 1822. This alliance made Kirkgate one of the largest markets in Europe. Later, stallholders were provided with their own air-raid shelter in the market during World War II and the Ministry of Food operated its ration plan from offices on the elegant balconies of the first floor.

The domes escaped damage when a huge fire engulfed a section of the market in December 1975 – Leeds' biggest fire disaster to date. Wear and tear took its toll on the domes and a planned refurbishment – including the domes – took a serious setback when, in 1992, another fire broke out, this time damaging the precious Leeming architecture. They were carefully restored to resemble their old selves during an overall renovation in 1996 and, thankfully, still provide a striking pose to the Leeds skyline today.

Address Vicar Lane, LS2 7HY | Getting there 1-minute walk from Leeds Bus Station or 8–10-minute walk from Leeds Railway Station | Hours Domes accessible 24 hours but opening hours to view the inside of the market are Mon–Sat 8am–5.30pm | Tip Check out the wide variety of traditional market stalls, as well as the diverse street food on offer towards the bottom of the indoor market. Alan Brown Florists is still trading after nearly 50 years in the market, and Teapot Café and Shop sources beverages from around the globe. Hollywood actor John Malkovich popped in one day during the filming of *Poirot* in nearby Saltaire.

46 Kirkstall Valley Trail

Its existence is a blessing!

Leeds is blessed with unexpected green oases dotted around its inner circles and urban boundaries, and Kirkstall Valley is perhaps one of the finest spots of all, which you will happily discover by taking a short pilgrimage from the city centre.

A walk, wheelchair ride or cycle along the Aire Valley Tow Path from Granary Wharf or Whitehall Road are perhaps the best ways to approach and appreciate the big and wonderful reveal of Kirkstall Valley. The path will brush past the impressive Leeds Industrial Museum at Armley Mills before introducing you to Brewery Mills, converted from the old brewery to accommodate the students of Leeds Beckett University. Locks, a marina, weirs and goits can all be spotted along the route. 'Goit' is a name peculiar to Yorkshire and Lancashire meaning a small water channel, many of which fed into the textile mills. Wyther Lane car park signals that if you want to immerse in the delights of Kirkstall Valley Nature Reserve, you had better leave the path here.

The reserve sits in 10 hectares of rejuvenated orchards, thanks to Yorkshire Wildlife Trust's efforts, and has plenty of healthy woodland, wetland and grassland, as well as being a home for a wide range of birds and wildlife. Head north from the reserve, passing The Bridge Inn, and you will catch a first glimpse through the trees of the mesmerising 12th-century Kirkstall Abbey, a well-known but still unmissable ecclesiastical landmark. The abbey's monks were some of the first people to prosper from the land, as they established their own tanneries, smithies, ironworks and corn mills. The chapter house, refectory, nave, cloister and abbot's lodgings are still in evidence, and the abbey is surrounded by acres of pleasant parkland. The abbey's gatehouse is famous for its fine museum, established in 1927, and includes a carefully observed replica of a typical Victorian street.

Address Abbey Road, Kirkstall, LS5 3EH | **Getting there** Bus 33, 34 or 757 to Abbey Walk; by car: take the A 65 towards Skipton from the city centre, through Kirkstall, and the abbey is situated on the left approximately 3 miles (4.8 kilometres) from the city centre | **Hours** Valley trail accessible 24 hours; Kirkstall Abbey Tue–Sun 10am–4pm | **Tip** Kirkstall Forge is the oldest continuously used industrial site in Leeds, dating back to the 12th century, and was a working ironworks during the 19th century. It is now a mixed commercial use site, and a railway station opened in 2016 to accommodate the commuters, close to the former railway that ran from 1860 to 1905.

47 Leeds Bridge
The site of the world's first moving pictures

Louis Le Prince's mysterious disappearance in 1890 is still the subject of much conspiratorial conjecture. Was he murdered at the hands of jealous rival, Thomas Edison, or killed by a money-grabbing brother? Did he commit suicide in a bid to hide the secret of his sexuality?

The fact is that in 1888 the Frenchman was the cinematographer who shot the first moving pictures in the world, and they were taken in two Leeds locations. Le Prince filmed them on Leeds Bridge and Roundhay Park using a single lens camera and a strip of paper for film. The Roundhay Park footage showed a group of people walking in a circle, but it is the Leeds Bridge footage of goods-laden carriages and pedestrians crossing that is arguably the most popular.

Forensic examinations revealed that the camera used in the footage taken by Le Prince showed an early version of the same mechanism used later in moving picture cameras by his rivals. It left experts in little doubt that Thomas Edison and the Lumière brothers were indeed not the first pioneers of cinematography and that Le Prince should lay claim to that.

Metz-born Le Prince moved to Leeds to refine his cinematic skills from a small workshop in Woodhouse. Leeds Bridge, at the foot of Briggate, was chosen as it was seen as a splendid example of Victorian engineering. It replaced the original wooden medieval bridge when that was destroyed. The cast iron road bridge, which bears the old Leeds Corporation coat of arms, was built in 1870 and was the location for the wool cloth market, marking it as the focal point for the hustle and bustle of city life.

Le Prince was due to address a meeting in New York about his projection techniques. He boarded a train in France shortly before his Atlantic journey but disappeared without trace. His great-great-granddaughter donated the film as a lasting legacy to the Leeds Philosophical and Literary Society.

Address Leeds Bridge, Bridge End Road, LS1 4DJ | Getting there Walk down Lower Briggate shopping street in the centre and cross to Bridge End Road where the bridge stands | Hours Accessible 24 hours | Tip Leeds Bridge House across the bridge on Hunslet Road is an interesting Grade II-listed corner dwelling built in 1875. The house was used as a viewing platform for people trying to get a better look at the film shot on the bridge that day.

48 Leeds Corn Exchange

An iconic beauty not to be missed

The Leeds Corn Exchange is one of the city's most iconic buildings, and it had been lying virtually abandoned and unloved for years until it was refurbished and reawakened in 2008. Its breath-taking, rejuvenated dome cradles an eclectic mix of independent shops, small restaurants and even a sculpture gallery, favouring the retail underdog instead of playing host to homogenised High Street stores.

The Corn Exchange, completed in 1863, was designed by Cuthbert Brodrick, who was also the architect of the equally stunning Leeds Town Hall. The design of the dome was inspired by the Bourse De Commerce in Paris, and the building housed the sack market and the sale of corn and wheat. Trade continued here right through to the 1950s, until a slow decline unjustly consigned the building to a shadow of its former self, with just a few offices remaining.

Today, independent businesses bring the Corn Exchange to life with their colourful façades decorating the upper and lower balconies. On the upper, the Sculpture Gallery showcases work by new sculptors and artists, in addition to pieces by a handful of creatives who own and run the gallery. OWT – a Yorkshire dialect word meaning 'anything' – is a family-run restaurant with a French connection. Owner Esther Miglio grew up in France and uses her knowledge of her family's wine business to educate the novice wine aficionados.

There is an abundance of treasures. Released Records offers new and pre-loved vinyls. NARR Radio is an independent station broadcasting from the Corn Exchange that draws on Leeds' rich history of post-punk and operates at weekends. Red Tattoo and Piercing and Mr Men's Barbershop serve up a spot of pampering, and there are lots of alternative fashion and jewellery businesses: choice is plentiful. The Great Yorkshire Shop even offers a citizen test and passport to sort out die-hard tykes among the 'johnny come lately' shoppers!

Address Call Lane, LS1 7BR, +44 (0)113 234 0363, www.leedscornexchange.co.uk, info@leedscornexchange.co.uk | Getting there A three-minute walk from Leeds Bus Station. Head up New York Street towards the city before turning on to Call Lane; from Leeds Railway Station, walk towards Boar Lane which leads directly to Leeds Corn Exchange | Hours Mon–Wed 10am–6pm, Thu 10am–9pm, Fri & Sat 10am–6pm, Sun 10.30am–4.30pm | Tip Nearby on Boar Lane you will find The Bankers' Cat, a pub selling craft beer. Although recently renovated, it has a traditional feel about it, complete with old-style pumps and mahogany bar. The old Chubb Bank vault in the basement has been preserved and is now a small party space.

49 The Leeds Hippo Bones

A reality, not fantasy

It has been described as one of the strangest discoveries in the city, but it is an historical accuracy that hippopotami did roam the lands around West Yorkshire.

The hippo bones can be viewed at Leeds City Museum where they take pride of place. They were discovered in 1852 at a brick and clay quarry – a site now occupied by the inner-city ring road, Armley Gyratory. They were taken at the time to Henry Denny, a curator with Leeds Philosophical and Literary Society Museum who then returned to the site to uncover more bones. He revealed the remains belonged to not one, but three Great Northern Hippopotami, an elephant and an auroch, an extinct type of wild ox.

The precise age of the bones was initially in doubt as they were first carbon dated to a period after the last Ice Age. This proved perplexing, as the cold tundra conditions would have meant it would have been impossible for the animals to survive during this particular period. But there was a flaw in the dating of these types of bones as, during the 19th century, scientists would often coat old bones in gelatine to preserve them. However, the substance in the gelatine reacted with the radiocarbon dating material, prompting an inaccurate result. A molar tooth from the hippo was finally tested and the remains were given a more realistic age of around 26,000 years old. This would have tallied with the occurrence of interglacial periods that brought more temperate climes in the North.

The hippo bones were displayed at Leeds Philosophical and Literary Museum and the story remained a hot topic of conversation for years. They even survived bombings in the city during World War II, which left other artefacts badly damaged. Sadly, they were left to gather dust when the museum in Bond Street finally closed in 1965. They were housed in various archives in Leeds until they reached their current home in the museum.

Address Millennium Square, LS2 8BH, +44 (0)113 378 5001, www.museumsandgalleries.leeds.gov.uk | Getting there Millennium Square is a 10-minute walk from Leeds Railway Station; head towards the Headrow from Park Row. It is a 15-minute walk from Leeds Bus Station; head towards Eastgate and the Headrow. | Hours Tue – Fri 10am – 5pm, Sat & Sun 11am – 5pm | Tip At Leeds City Museum you can also visit the 3,000-year-old mummified remains of Nesyamun, an Egyptian priest in the Egyptian Room on the upper floor. The remains lie in a coffin that is on permanent display.

50 Leeds Irish Centre
Providing a taste of home

Around 50,000 of Leeds' population are of Irish descent, and 2020 marked half a century since the grand opening of Leeds Irish Centre.

The centre opened in response to a cry from immigrants to the city in need of an Irish home-from-home, providing cultural familiarities to which they were used and dearly missed. Most of the migrants came to the city from Ireland in the second half of the 20th century to swell the numbers required for Britain's social and economic recovery in the aftermath of World War II. Smaller clubs existed prior to 1970 in and around Leeds but when Councillor Michael Rooney secured three acres of land in York Road, a central, purpose-built club finally offered the facilities under one roof.

Today, the Irish Centre is carefully managed by a group of trustees and is home to 1,150 members and those without Irish blood are also wholly welcome. It offers traditional Irish cultural events providing a grand craic for young and old such as dancing, folk music and Gaelic sports as well as live music, concerts, food, quizzes, bingo, comedy … the list is endless. There are four function rooms and even an outdoor recreational field. It is also a popular venue for weddings and parties but equally important, the club is a focal point for vulnerable and lonely people seeking company and advice.

The Fall famously played a live gig to a packed crowd in 2005 at Leeds Irish Centre, coinciding with their newly released *Fall Heads Roll* album. House of Love played in 1988 before a much more intimate crowd but the late broadcaster, John Peel, opined it was one of the best he had seen.

Still a ubiquitous part of Leeds Irish Centre is Tommy McLoughlin a one-time manager and DJ at the centre who remains a die-hard member. Tommy – whose family hails from County Mayo – is never far from the action, so you might just spot him on the dance floor at the next ceilidh.

Address York Road, LS9 9NT, +44 (0)113 248 0887, theleedsirishcentre.co.uk | **Getting there** Bus 19A, 40, 56 or 64 to York Road / Raincliffe Road; by car: take the A 64 road towards York out of the city centre where you will find it after a short drive at the corner of York Road and Temple View Road | **Hours** Open 7 days a week but opening times depending on different functions vary, so it is advisable to call or check the website | **Tip** Nearby Killingbeck Cemetery is a Roman Catholic burial ground filled with monuments and war memorials, and is the final resting place for many of Leeds' Irish community.

51 The Leeds Library

'We never knew you were here'

The 18th-century writer, James Boswell, once wrote: 'In Leeds, where one would not expect it, there is a very good public library where strangers are greeted with great civility.' Still in existence today, sandwiched in the commercial hub of one of the busiest shopping streets in the city, The Leeds Library is a true hidden gem.

From the outside, one would hardly realise it exists but once you enter its magnificent TARDIS-like walls, it leaves an indelible mark. It is like entering a different world, leaving behind the cacophonous madness on the street, to a soothing feeling of well-being.

Founded in 1768, The Leeds Library is one of the oldest existing independent subscription libraries in the country, pre-dating public libraries. The building it calls home today – designed by Thomas Johnson in the Greek Revival style – opened in 1808 and today has more than 1,000 members. By sheer coincidence, over 1,000 books are added to its collection each year.

The original staircases and balustrades provide natural beautiful frames for the books, old and new, and the building even boasts its own bookworm ghost, often heard whiffling around the balconies of the library late at night. Membership is by subscription and anyone over the age of 18 with a permanent address can apply. Members are treated to a wealth of knowledge courtesy of literature of all kinds. The oldest book, *The Book of Marvels and Travels*, by Sir John Mandeville, dates back to 1494.

The library has a strong leaning towards 18th- and 19th-century travel, fiction, history, science and periodicals. However, fans of modernity will not be disappointed with the provision of audio books and more contemporary literature.

Limited opening times mean that a sneaky peak at the library is by appointment for non-members but Boswell is right about one thing: strangers will indeed be greeted with great civility.

Address 18 Commercial Street, LS1 6AL, +44 (0)113 245 3071, www.theleedslibrary.org.uk |
Getting there 5-minute walk from both Leeds Bus Station and Leeds Railway Station down
the pedestrianised shopping street | Hours By appointment only Mon–Wed 9.30am–6pm,
Thu & Fri 9.30am–7pm, Sat 9.30am–1.30pm; free twice-monthly tours; every Thu public
opening 5–7pm | Tip The British Library at Boston Spa, Wetherby, has a large selection of
periodicals, sound recordings, micro film and three centuries of newspapers, all perfect for
research purposes.

52 Leeds Liverpool Canal's First Lock

One down, just another 90 to go!

The Leeds Liverpool Canal is a superb piece of civil engineering and today remains the longest of its kind in Britain. The first lock, marking the start of its 127-mile (204-kilometre) zigzag journey, can be found in the heart of the city.

The lock serves as a sort of hand-over at the spot where the waters from the Aire and Calder Navigation merge cleanly with the Leeds Liverpool Canal's premier point; a deliberate piece of engineering to join the east of England with the west. The canal then takes over the waterway's west wing, meandering towards its final destination at Liverpool's Stanley Docks.

Plans for the construction of the canal were hatched in a Bradford pub by merchants and engineers in 1766. They wanted to link the industrial towns of the North that were then the engine rooms of the Industrial Revolution. In an age that pre-dated railways, canals were essential infrastructures for transporting the goods to destinations throughout Britain. Commodities such as coal were especially vital to keep the factory cogs turning.

It took more than 50 years to build the entire canal but the first section was opened between Bingley and Skipton in 1773 making great use of the treasure of limestone in the Yorkshire Dales for construction purposes. The lengthy negotiations and the limp to the final 91st lock were complex. Wrangling over the route, high taxes, the Napoleonic Wars, illnesses and sudden deaths of the major players in the project, were just a few of the delay factors.

The Leeds Liverpool Canal remained a vital artery for the transportation of goods well into the 20th century. During World War II it served as a defence against the bombings, still in evidence today, as pill boxes and blockhouses pepper different stretches of its journey.

Address Canal Wharf, LS11 5PS | **Getting there** Walk under the Dark Arches on Neville Street and head for the Water Lane Boathouse. The lock is directly next to it. | **Hours** Accessible 24 hours | **Tip** The former canal boathouse known as Water Lane Boathouse has been renovated and is now a lovely pub and restaurant selling hearty fare. Plenty of outdoor seating ensures customers get the best of the views of the canal and lock.

53 The Leeds Loins

'A place of shelter from the wind and the rain'

What do you call a person from Leeds? 'Leedscunion' or 'Leedsudlian' don't have quite the same ring to them. But what about 'Loiner'? A Leeds Loiner is indeed the correct alliterative name for a native. After much speculation, it has been assumed the word 'loiner' is an elongated version of the city's unique alleyways, known as 'loins' or 'low ins'. They can be found lurking between the shops, waiting to take you from one street to another. The name of these passageways may often confuse visitors to the city, as the thoroughfares hold other colloquialisms: 'ginnel' to those in West Yorkshire, and 'gennel', if you don't mind, to Sheffield people and their kind.

The loins provide most suitable cobbled accommodation to three historic little 17th- and 18th-century pubs in upper Briggate: The Packhorse, Angel Inn and The Ship serve proper ales and unpretentious hearty pies, more suited to places where you would find shelter from the wind and rain. The pubs have hung around these parts for years, and are now pushed aside a little by the swanky bars and restaurants.

Ignore the loins pubs at your peril, for they carry an inordinate amount of history, and are thought to be the only timber-framed buildings left in the city. The Packhorse, dating back to 1615, was reputed to have entertained Royalist soldiers during the English Civil War. The Angel Inn was the watering hole where John Aspdin sold his newly invented Portland Cement. The Ship once stood on a medieval manorial boundary known as a 'burbage plot', and The Packhorse still bears a cross of the Knights' Templar, a military arm of the Catholic church.

The little bits of history found in these pubs are best seen by escaping the jostle at the bar and heading upstairs to admire the wooden beams and panelling. Great actors and writers have enjoyed a drink or two in the Leeds loins. The late Peter O'Toole was a fan!

Address Upper Briggate, LS1 6LN | Getting there Bus 4, 7, 16 or 16A to Boar Lane then a 5-minute walk. The pubs can be found on the left-hand side of the northern end of Briggate if you head towards The Headrow. | Tip The White Swan, Swan Street, is also an historic pub in Leeds, dating back to 1748. It can be found not quite in a loin but a yard that it shares with the famous City Varieties Music Hall.

54__The Leeds Pals Memorial
A peaceful resting place of remembrance

A beauty spot on a remote hillside in North Yorkshire may seem an odd location for a memorial to the 'Leeds Pals', but uncover the back story and it makes sound sense.

The Leeds Pals Memorial is a stone cairn, decorated with the York Rose and ring-fenced to capture the eye of the pilgrim to Breary Banks in the heart of the Yorkshire Dales. It opened in 1933 and stands as a sombre tribute to the soldiers of the West Yorkshire Regiment 15th Battalion. The Leeds regiment was one of 96 'pals' troops in Britain during World War I, formed by Lord Kitchener. The 'pals' were recruited from groups of friends, neighbours and family members in a bid to raise camaraderie and spirits during appalling conflicts.

Breary Banks at Colsterdale provided a quiet calm for the training troops before the terrible storm of the combats. Relatives and friends, who spent their own savings to build the memorial, deemed the location a peaceful antithesis to the horrors their loved ones witnessed in battle.

The Leeds Pals left North Yorkshire to fight in Egypt with the purpose of defending the Suez Canal in 1916. But they were quickly seconded to Northern France after countless casualties left huge shortages in combat troops. The defence of the village of Serre in the Somme valley, became a particularly deep bloodbath as Allied soldiers were ambushed and decimated by German machine guns. Out of the 750 Leeds Pals fighting, 248 were killed instantly and hundreds more were wounded over five days. Throughout the four years of conflict, 1,861 men lost their lives and hundreds more were wounded or were missing in battle from this one West Yorkshire regiment.

Two of the Leeds Pals who lived beyond the war, Walter Hare and Herbert Verrity, gave an account of their experiences, and their voices were posthumously used – along with others – in Peter Jackson's 2018 film *They Shall Not Grow Old*.

Address Breary Banks, Colsterdale near Masham, HG4 4NN | Getting there Dales bus services to Masham; check the website for details, www.dalesbus.org; by car: take the A 65 towards Skipton then the A 61 towards Ripon before heading on to the A 6108 towards Leyburn. At Masham, follow the single-track road to Colsterdale, or take the A 1 North junction 50 for Ripon and pick up the A 61 (A 6108). A small car park is provided next to the River Burn. | Hours Accessible 24 hours | Tip George Edwin Ellison, a miner from Leeds, was the last British man to die in action during World War I. He was killed at Mons in Belgium on 11 November, 1918 just 90 minutes before the armistice was signed. A plaque tribute to him can be found at Leeds Railway Station.

55 The Leeds Skyline

A tale of two cities

The ever-changing skyline of Leeds is probably best observed on the Doubletree by Hilton's 13th floor. It is here, in the hotel's public bar and restaurant, that you will discover one of the best panoramic views over a tale of two cities.

Peering out over the southern end of Leeds, vistas can be enjoyed from the outside terrace – acrophobia permitting – of the former print and woollen mills of Holbeck, Middleton, Beeston and Hunslet. Many of them have been given a brush and clean in readiness for slick digital media types. A clear view of skylit rooftops gives a clear hint that these were once textile mills that housed grazing sheep awaiting a 'haircut' to provide the much-needed wool. Rothwell's historic St George's Clock Tower can be seen at 11am, at roughly 1pm you can catch a glimpse of Morley Town Hall, but the ubiquitously sighted cooling towers of Ferrybridge Power Station were demolished in 2019, leaving a more rural landscape to the east. The modern high-rise 'Dalek' building is the black sheep in an otherwise heritage-laden urban view.

Cross to the other side of the bar and a different picture awaits on the northern skyline. Only interior shots are provided here, and the image awaiting is one of giant cranes and Legoed structures of half-built skyscrapers. The university's clock tower defiantly craves attention in a sea of modernity.

Heavy financial investment here will radically transform the northern views over the city, and it has already begun with the building of Altus House, a 38-storey skyscraper, soon to be Leeds' tallest landmark, providing student accommodation and amenities in Lovell Park Road and Merrion Way. Leeds Beckett's new school of art building will also be reaching for the skies. But for the nostalgic among you, enjoy the views on the south side: a 23-storey tower block will soon be about to join the 'old uns' on Globe Road.

Address Doubletree by Hilton, Granary Wharf, 2 Wharf Approach, LS1 4BR, +44 (0)113 241 1000, www.leedsskylounge.com | Getting there From Leeds Railway Station, use the South Entrance (Holbeck Urban Village) and walk through the Dark Arches: the hotel is straight in front | Hours Mon–Thu 8–1am, Fri 8–2am, Sat 7–2am, Sun 7–1am | Tip If you look towards the very top of 'The Dalek' from the south-side terrace, you might see the family of buzzards that were spotted nest making in their new city home. The birds of prey normally frequent heavily wooded areas. These buzzards are said to enjoy the commute from the city to nearby woods.

56 __ Left Bank Leeds

An open door without barriers

Folk have a habit of overusing the clichéd phrase 'When one door closes, another one opens', but if applied metaphorically to Left Bank Leeds, it couldn't be more true. This unique registered charity has resurrected the former St Margaret of Antioch Church in Cardigan Road, while respectfully preserving its original heritage.

This is a place of marvels, and it was thanks to a group of Christians who rescued it from decay that it is alive and well today. It is a multidisciplinary arts space that opens its doors (original) to humanist weddings, co-working space, films, live music, opera, festivals, workshops – the list is endless. Even those who just want to take a pew and sit with a hot drink and a cake can come to the regular afternoon tea parties organised here, and small art exhibitions in the porch gallery are held each week.

The church opened in 1909 to serve the Anglican congregation living in newly built terraced cottages nearby, but closed its doors in 1985 when it merged with a nearby parish. St Margaret's roof was almost destroyed in the intervening years, and English Heritage was persuaded to pay for urgent repairs. After much discussion over its future purpose, Left Bank reopened the doors in 2001. The church is now Grade II* listed – the star signifies it is of special importance – and has given a bit of humanist art and soul back to the people.

Every corner of the church has a purpose, even the lovely front garden, which is used for functions. Worship may no longer take place, but respect for St Margaret's interior is maintained. It is still very much the imposing brick-built neo-gothic structure it once was. Inside, light floods in through the stained-glass rose windows and the oak choir stalls remain as they were. The robing room is home to a fridge freezer now, but its oak studded arched door and the grand columns are not going anywhere. The overall aim is to inspire and empower those who open this sacred door.

Address 143 Cardigan Road, LS6 1LG, +44 (0)113 278 5822, www.leftbankleeds.org.uk |
Getting there Bus 19 or 19A to Cardigan Road; or train to Burley Park Station and a
5-minute walk | Hours Wed 10am–5pm; pay-what-you-feel afternoon tea second Wed of
each month 2–3.30pm; check website for details of other events | Tip East Street Arts,
St Mary's Lane in Leeds 9, was formed by Karen Watson and Jon Wakeman. It is also a
charity and gives opportunity and support to contemporary artists.

57 Leonora Cohen's House

A 'tower' of strength in the suffragette movement

'Deeds, not words', was one of the mantras of the suffragette movement, and perhaps no equality campaigner remained as faithful to this ethos as did Leonora Cohen. At first glance, her former home nestles, just like any other, among a host of handsome terraces in Little Woodhouse. On closer inspection, an inscription on its solid front, courtesy of Leeds Civic Trust, provides a tribute to one remarkable former occupant.

Leonora Cohen came to national prominence in 1913, after being dubbed the 'Tower Suffragette' in the aftermath of her arrest at the Tower of London's Jewel House, when she seized the chance to smash the glass case holding the Insignia of Merit. She was later acquitted but was arrested for her protests on two other occasions, even embarking on a period of hunger strike at one point. She was later awarded the Hunger Strike Medal 'For Valour'. Possessing a strong moral code, Leonora did not believe in displays of violence on 'innocent' members of the public, and vented her protest only on government heads.

She was born Leonora Throp in Hunslet in 1873 and was raised by her widowed mother, whom she credited with instilling her beliefs – largely through witnessing her financial struggles. She married outside her own faith after meeting Henry Cohen, a Jewish jeweller's assistant and the couple lived in Little Woodhouse with their son, Reginald, for many years. In 1909, Leonora joined the Women's Social and Political Movement which led the suffragette campaign. She lobbied for women's equality in the workplace, her efforts being especially prodigious during employment at a local munitions factory in World War I. In the intervening years, when some women were given the vote between 1918 and 1928, she was the first woman to be called to the magistrate's bench and served as a JP for 25 years. She was awarded an OBE in 1928 and died in 1978, aged 105.

Address 2 Claremont Villas, Little Woodhouse, LS2 9NY | **Getting there** Bus 5 to Clarendon Road/Woodhouse Square; on foot, a short walk from Leeds General Infirmary, passing St George's Crypt, crossing the bridge and heading to Clarendon Road. Claremont Villas is adjacent to Clarendon Road. | **Hours** Viewable from the outside only | **Tip** You can learn more on the life of Leonora Cohen at Leeds City Museum, Millennium Square, which houses interesting artefacts belonging to the suffragette.

58 Leventhorpe Vineyard

À votre santé, love!

A vineyard on the edge of Leeds seems like a far-fetched concept, but history suggests that wine growing in this northern city goes back as far as the Romans and the Cistercian monks in the grounds of the local Kirkstall Abbey.

When chemist George Bowden chose to take a rural route on a winter's day from East Leeds to Wakefield, it was a decision that changed his life. George was driving on the long and winding Bullerthorpe Lane, linking Temple Newsam to the village of Woodlesford, and idly looked across at a snow-covered field for sale. A few hours later and the return journey painted a different picture. George observed the snow had all but gone, and what was more, no melting water appeared on the land. He immediately set the wheels in motion to buy the self-draining, south-facing five-acre site and 35 years later … one of Britain's most northerly vineyards is still thriving in the ancient wine-growing tradition in Leeds.

George and Janet Bowden are at the helm of Leventhorpe Vineyard, which has counted Leeds-born artist, Damien Hurst and musician, Liam Gallagher, among its wine-tasting visitors. Wine lovers are welcome to take a little tipple of the local award-winning Leventhorpe Sparkling, and Madeleine Angevine – which can be arranged by appointment. The Bowden connoisseurs are more than willing to give the uninitiated a lesson in matching the correct wine with the right foods. Visitors can also watch the process of vino making from the vine to the bottle in George's compact wine fermenting on-site workshop, and can order a bottle or four if they so wish; though no pressure.

Leventhorpe's reputation was sealed not just on the tables of Yorkshire but in vin-loving France. The wines, coupled with special Yorkshire cheeses, were presented at the finish line of the Tour de France at the Champs-Elysées in Paris following the cycle race in 2012.

Address Newsam Green Road, Bullerthorpe Lane, Woodlesford, LS26 8AF, +44 (0)113 288 9088, www.leventhorpevineyard.co.uk | **Getting there** Bus 167 or 168, get off between Woodlesford and Swillington on the A 642; by car, take the M 62 junction 30 exit and head through the village of Oulton that merges with Woodlesford on the A 642 towards Garforth | **Hours** Mon–Sat 11am–4pm, Sun noon–4pm | **Tip** At Woodlesford you will find Woodlesford and Lemon Royd Lock on the Aire and Calder Navigation. This is a little hidden beauty spot cultivated with flowers and trees. There is a lovely walk along the canal to the marina at Fleet Lane, Oulton.

59 The Lifting Tower

Still a handsome railway landmark from a bygone age

Was this once the gateway to a besieged castle, or could it have been a fair maiden's lookout folly? Even some locals are unaware of its history, but the answer is neither of these. Peeping behind a curtain of modern high-rise offices in Wellington Place, the Lifting Tower is a great Victorian remnant from the Yorkshire, Lancashire, London and North Western Railways. It is now splendidly repaired, though bereft of its original beating mechanisms. It stands today proud and alone on the site of the former goods station of the old Leeds Central railway station, which stood on this site for 120 years. It was unveiled to show its new grandeur in 2011 after local business promoters, MEPC, rescued it.

It used to be one of two such towers built in the 1850s to hoist the wagons from the viaduct into the goods yard below, and it was one of the last in the country to cease working and indeed to survive when it finally wound down in the 1970s. It was no longer needed when the city's new railway station opened in 1967 at its present New Station Street address.

It is coated in yellow sandstone and gritstone, and in its heyday this lifting tower and its twin had two platforms, one operating by a pulley system at ground level and the other at the viaduct. If one load was much heavier than the other, steam power assisted and guaranteed the safe landing of the carriages.

The area surrounding the lifting tower is now supremely land-scaped as if to give a ta-da moment to the tower, surprising local workers and visitors as they spy it for the first time. Interior coloured lights have even been placed to give it an extra sparkle as a conso-lation for the long-departed machinery. Entrepreneurs have made tentative enquiries as to its availability since its renaissance but for now it enjoys a fairy tale ending in splendid isolation – well, save for a fair few modern offices.

Address Wellington Place, LS1 4AP, between Whitehall Road and Wellington Street |
Getting there Bus 4, 16, 33, 54, 65, 229 or 255 to Whitehall Road or Wellington Street |
Hours Accessible 24 hours | Tip Across the way on Whitehall Road was the site of the
old Joseph Watson and Sons' Whitehall Soap works, affectionately known as 'Soapy Joe's',
one of the largest in England. A restaurant – The Soap Factory – is now on the site at
4 Whitehall Quay.

60__Little Woodhouse

A walk around here will do you good

In 1715, Little Woodhouse was described by historian Ralph Thoresby as 'one of the pleasantest hamlets in our parish', and thanks to its proud residents the area has held onto this reputation, despite being swallowed into the mouth of LS post codes. The grand cloth mills and mansions may have been adjusted to suit modernity, but appearances have hardly altered. They remain fiercely protected by Little Woodhouse Community Association, whose members fight to keep the buildings and gardens out of harm's way from greedy developers.

A walk around Little Woodhouse is a privilege, and the association members have thoughtfully drawn up maps and give regular talks on their charge. The circuit starts with the grand St George's Church whose 13th-century façade remains, though the church steeple did blow down during a storm in 1962. The walk then takes you past the former infirmary, St George's Crypt, built as a refuge centre for the destitute, which is still a shelter for the homeless; then the Edwardian splendour of Swarthmore, a small college today, and former home of Quaker, George Fox. The path bows to the statue of Sir Peter Fairbairn, founder of one of Leeds' first textile mills. He was knighted by Queen Victoria, once a house guest of a friend in Little Woodhouse.

Head up to the pretty Woodhouse Square, built to smoke screen the smog-filled air and soot-laden chimneys on the horizon. Hanover Square is awash with trees and flowers and stands before the elegant 1786 Denison Hall, built for wealthy heir, John Denison; his prior residence is now home to luxury apartments. The walk also brushes with grand 18th-century homes like Claremont, Waverley House and 11 Hanover Square, but also meanders into the narrow, sometimes cobbled, streets such as Little Woodhouse Street and Chorley Lane – homes for the mill and textile grafters; still sturdy cottages today.

Address St George's Church, Great George Street, LS1 3BR (start of the walk),
www.littlewoodhouseonline.com | Getting there Bus 5 to Woodhouse Square / Clarendon
Road | Hours Accessible 24 hours | Tip The former St Michael's College just out of the
walk's route on St John's Road – known locally as 'St Mick's' – is a former Jesuit Priests'
school built in 1905 by Benedict Williamson. It was closed in the 1970s, but its façade and
statue of St Michael remain fully on show. It was turned into bijou flats occupied by young
professionals who share the communal gardens.

61 Live at Leeds

'The most explosive live album ever made'

Walk through the University of Leeds' entrance gates and you immediately join another world where a vast crowd of mostly loquacious 'young uns' envelope the pleasant grounds. Saunter straight ahead and there, on the left, might look like just your average student refectory, but its walls contain a small piece of embedded rock history. A plaque, high on the wall, attests that it was here on 14 February, 1970 that probably the greatest rock album of all time was recorded by four young men from London: Roger Daltrey, Pete Townshend, John Entwistle and Keith Moon – otherwise known as The Who – chose this humble venue. They recorded the eponymous *Live at Leeds*, which remains, to this day, a rock classic.

After touring the US, The Who – who were known to be arguably the best live band around at the time – wanted to create an authentic homespun album to be recorded in Leeds and Hull on the following day, as a follow-up (and antidote) to *Tommy*, which was becoming a bit of a millstone for them. A technical failure meant it was curtains for Hull's plans and so Leeds was the sole chosen one.

The refectory is pretty big, but on the day of recording, a small corner was sealed off to allow in just 2,000 adoring fans. Not much has altered in the refectory since then, but its significance transcends all of that. The modest stage stands at one end of the refectory and, at the other, a kitchen serving a selection of reasonably priced fayre. Out of the 34 songs recorded, just 6 were on the album, including *See Me, Feel Me, Substitute* and a 15-minute version of *My Generation*. The album reached number 3 in the charts at the time.

The refectory's walls are adorned with endless lists of line-ups who have played there from the 1960s right up to the present day. It's like a who's who in rock gods: Jimi Hendrix, Led Zeppelin, The Clash, Pink Floyd … but The Who will always remain Leeds' chosen ones.

Address University of Leeds, Woodhouse Lane, LS2 9JT, +44 (0)113 243 1751, www.leeds.ac.uk | **Getting there** Bus 1, 6, 28 or 56 to Parkinson Building Steps or a 20-minute walk from the City Square | **Hours** Mon–Fri 8am–7pm, Sat & Sun 10am–2pm (but reduced hours outside of term time) | **Tip** The Dry Dock, opposite the University's Parkinson Building on Woodhouse Lane, is a quirky pub in the form of a disused boat docked on a piece of land. It offers local beers and tasty food.

62 Lost and Found

What a lovely way to spend a penny!

Leeds never fails to throw surprises at you. The oak-panelled drawing rooms of the grandiose clubs frequented by wealthy industrialists and the bourgeoisie, are slowly being restored to their former glory. City buildings, once ignored as has-beens, are head-turners now. The Lost and Found on Albion Place is enjoying its day in the sun once more, and it is a dazzling place to be, even when forced to spend a penny!

The former Victorian gentlemen's club opened in 1849, and was built for William Hey (1736–1819), esteemed Chief Surgeon at Leeds General Infirmary for 50 years. The aim of the club was to provide a networking sanctuary for rich mill and factory workers, eminent medics and general top brass of industrial Northern society of the time. The club boasted dining rooms, billiard tables and even bedrooms. A secret bar could also be found, but that still remains hush-hush.

The club is now a restaurant and bar, in keeping with modern demands, but the architects must be applauded for their sensitive and painstaking research, as the Victorian features have been polished and treasured. The beautiful ornate cornicing, columned fireplaces and original sweeping oak staircases give a very royal welcome to those who enter. Perhaps the biggest surprise is the ladies' toilets, which should be greatly admired, and even those who are not caught short should take a look. To greet you is plush velvet seating with a ground-to-ceiling golden mirror. The walls are awash with suitable Victorian colour schemes and subtle lighting. Enter the 'business end' and you merge into a world of regal splendour with marble sink tops, gleaming brass taps and porcelain sinks, and yet more elegant seating areas. The cubicles have more efficient versions of the old pull chain flushes, but otherwise they are uncanny *doppelgängers* of the original urinals – minus the gentlemen of course!

Address 3 Albion House, LS1 6JL, +44 (0)113 493 1450, www.the-lostandfound.co.uk |
Getting there Albion Place can be found between Lands Lane and Albion Street in the
city centre, just off one of the main shopping areas, Commercial Street | **Hours** Sun–Wed
10am–11pm, Thu 10am–midnight, Fri & Sat 10–1am | **Tip** Next door to the Lost
and Found is Bill's Restaurant, which is also housed in an historic Victorian setting and
beautifully restored. This was once the first building of the Yorkshire College.

63__The Lost Chilean Mural
A thank you of solidarity and friendship

This piece of 40-year-old historical artwork was nearly lost in 2017 when renovation began in Leeds University's Woodhouse Campus. Hidden in a seemingly innocuous wall, the peeling plaster revealed a tiny corner of the Chilean national flag. This was, in fact, a small part of a far bigger picture: a hand-painted Chilean mural. It was a gift from students and activists who had lovingly hand painted it after fleeing the civil war in Chile in the early 1970s, then under the dictatorship of Augusto Pinochet. They wanted to show their unstinting gratitude to the many people of Leeds who had accepted them with loving arms. Their exile was seen as necessary, as an estimated 30,000 Chileans were killed or mysteriously disappeared during the regime and thousands more tortured by followers of Pinochet's military junta.

The colourful mural – painted in 1976 – was carefully restored to its former glory thanks to Heritage Lottery funding and the supervision of expert, Kasia Breska, along with members of the Chilean community of Leeds. The painting depicts miners and agricultural workers; a defiant protest by those forced to abandon their homes and jobs.

The words: 'Y habrá trabajo para todo' at the head of the mural are thoughtfully translated into English by its creators at the foot of the painting: *And there will be work for all*. It was a bold message to the oppressors in their home country but, conversely, a symbol of solidarity and friendship towards their adopted Leeds. It now stands encased in glass but can be carefully viewed by appointment.

Many refugees stayed in Leeds rather than return home, despite Pinochet being toppled in 1990. They have since built up a group in the city forming their own Chilean community. One of the original painters – Gilberto Hernandez – still lives in Leeds, and was there to witness the unveiling of the finished painting in 2018.

Address University of Leeds main campus, Woodhouse Lane, LS2 1JT, +44 (0)113 243 1751, www.leeds.ac.uk, mural@luu.org.uk | **Getting there** Bus 1, 6, 28 or 56 to Parkinson Building steps | **Hours** Phone or email for an appointment | **Tip** The Edit Room is a grab-and-go café in the newly refurbished Edward Boyle Library on Cromer Road, offering great food for all, including those with food allergies and intolerances.

64 The Lost Miniature Railway

Clues to a hidden past

Golden Acre Park, sandwiched between Bramhope and Adel, is 137 acres of green open spaces, woodland and landscaped gardens, which makes it a pleasant spot for families wanting an escape from the bustle of the city. It wasn't always like this, as it once had a brief encounter with a lavish amusement park. Tangible memories were virtually lost in the mists of time, apart from one little gem.

A tiny section of the park's railway is a reminder to a racy past, after parts of it were uncovered in 2003. These were the only remnants left of the park's miniature railway that once circumnavigated Golden Acre and was an integral piece of the fun. It was the drive needed to recreate a tiny replica – original parts included – of the railway. It can be found in front of the park café, as a sort of homage to the time it was alive on this earth. The theme park was the dream of Frank Thompson who wanted to rival Blackpool's Pleasure Beach. It opened in 1932 and included a lagoon, a water chute, a large central dance hall, monorails, motor boats and even hydroplanes. The miniature railway covered a huge distance around the lake, and it had two operating trains pulling open-top carriages. It was so popular the actress, Dame Anna Neagle, arrived one day for the unveiling of a new train. The theme park's design was modelled on a similar one on New York's Coney Island.

Cash problems and an impending conflict in mainland Europe led to its rather premature closure in 1938. It was left to fall into disrepair and the rides were dismantled and shipped elsewhere with only tiny traces of border fences left to testify a life once lived. The local council stepped in and bought Golden Acre – named after the colour of the stone once quarried here – and a more peaceful existence has since resumed.

Address Otley Road, Bramhope, LS16 8BQ, +44 (0)113 261 0374 | **Getting there**
Bus X 84 towards Skipton to The Parkway Hotel; by car: take the A 660 Otley Road from
Leeds city centre and turn off where you see the signs for the park near to The Parkway
Hotel | **Hours** Accessible 24 hours | **Tip** In the neighbouring suburb of Horsforth, you
will find a lovely little-known gem on The Green: Horsforth Village Museum. It is full of
interesting artefacts from bygone days of Horsforth, which was once described as the largest
village in Leeds before it became a suburb. The museum is open from March to September
at weekends.

65 — The Makkah Mosque

A place where everyone is welcome

In 2017, an imam and a rabbi from Leeds reenacted a famous scene from the film *Love Actually*, in response to the murder of MP, Jo Cox. Side by side, they silently held up written cards that showed a strong commonality between the two religions, often viewed as poles apart. Esther Hugenholtz of Sinai Synagogue of Leeds and Qari Asim of the Makkah Mosque were taking part in the 'Great Together' campaign established by Jo's family.

Qari Asim MBE is imam of the striking Makkah Masjid Mosque, in the Brudenell suburb. The mosque peeps out over the terraced houses in LS 6 and has won awards, not only for its stunning dome and bold stripes, but for the openness and respect to the wider community, spearheaded by the imam. Qari is a determined campaigner of causes such as tackling Islamophobia, welcoming those from all faiths wishing to view the mosque. Volunteers like Hanif are at hand to explain the subtleties of Muslim worship and the beauty of the mosque itself.

The mosque was purpose-built in 2003 on the site of a dilapidated wooden chapel, as the need to accommodate the burgeoning worshippers, who had outgrown the makeshift end-of-terrace houses nearby, had become a matter of urgency. The number of people wishing to worship at the mosque had risen to a staggering 3,000. Most of the Asian immigrants came to Leeds from the Indian sub-continent seeking work and had been joined by their extended family, which led to the swollen numbers. Some sold their inherited gold and silver to pay for the build, others gave their earnings and many organised fundraising events. Calligrapher Naveed Bhatti travelled from Pakistan to painstakingly hand-paint the different chapters of the Quran – the holy book of Islam – on the dome's ceiling. These are intricately written in Quranic Arabic, a language spoken in Mecca, and Naveed took a gruelling six months to complete the task.

Address 36 Thornville Road, LS6 1JY, +44 (0)7813 797213, www.makkahmosque.co.uk | **Getting there** Bus 19 or 56 from Vicar Lane, York Street and Woodhouse Lane; by car: from Woodhouse Lane, head towards Cardigan Road then turn right onto Harold Grove, leading to Thornville Road | **Hours** Accessible 24 hours | **Tip** On the next street from the mosque, on Harold Grove, is a terraced house with a white door, which is the childhood home of Spice Girl Melanie Brown.

66 Marks and Spencer

A penny for his thoughts led to fame and fortune

Write any story on the history of Leeds and it is unthinkable to omit Marks and Spencer, who from humble beginnings in the city built the worldwide empire we all know today.

Their story is celebrated with a bit of potted history around Leeds, starting with a celebratory M and S stall in Kirkgate Market where it all began, and ending at the Marks and Spencer Company Archive. A young Michal Marks left his home in Russian partitioned Poland in 1882 during the height of the pogroms. Born to Polish-Jewish parents, Marks arrived in Leeds penniless and promptly sought work for Barran clothing, which sold some of the first off-the-peg items in Britain, and was committed to employing Jewish immigrants to the city. It was Barran's trading with Leeds haberdasher, Isaac Dewhirst, that led to a double piece of good fortune for Marks. He bought goods from Dewhirst to sell independently and the profits enabled him to rent a stall in Kirkgate's outdoor market where the phrase 'Don't ask the price, it's a penny' was coined. This success led him to seek a business partner; step forward Dewhirst's cashier, Tom Spencer, to complete the start of the meteoric rise.

The stall – historical in appearance but not an exact replica of the first ever M and S stand that opened in 1904 – sells a variety of treats and sweets. From there you can easily walk to landmarks in the city, including the former Dewhirst warehouse where the two men first met. Head to the beautiful Cross Arcade, which opened in 1904 and housed further M and S shops during the early 1900s, before paying a visit to the M and S flagship Briggate store, which began trading in 1909. This can all be rounded off with a walk to Victoria Gardens on The Headrow, a green space funded by M and S.

The purpose-built Marks and Spencer Company Archive opened its doors on campus at the University of Leeds in 2000, and includes exhibitions of the brand's clothing and wares throughout the years.

Address Michael Marks Building, Western Campus, Clarendon Road, LS2 9LP, +44 (0)208 718 2800 or Kirkgate Market, Vicar Lane, LS2 7HY, www.marksintime.marksandspencer.com | **Getting there** For the Archive, bus 26 to Clarendon Road; on foot, it is a 15–20-minute walk from Leeds Railway Station | **Hours** Mon–Fri 10am–5pm; hours for Kirkgate Market Mon–Sat 8am–5.30pm | **Tip** As well as enabling you to find out the history of M and S, the Reading Room at the Michael Marks Building offers over 71,000 archived items including photographs, special collections, documents, VHS and DVDs, and details of the roles and stories of former employees.

67 Meanwood Valley Trail
A 'necessity, not a luxury'

The American writer, Edward Abbey, once said: 'Wilderness is not a luxury but a necessity of the human spirit.' This comes to mind when taking the Meanwood Valley Trail, a golden picture in touching distance from urban life but instilling a sense of mirthful wonderment when immersed in its glory.

It begins at Woodhouse Moor, close to the universities, with the 1878 statue of Henry Marsden, philanthropist and a mayor of Leeds, pointing the way. The trail covers 7 miles (11 kilometres) of spectacular wood and grassland until its final resting place at Adel's Golden Acre Park. It is described as a 'green artery' of the city, and visitors can walk the whole trail, or sections of it; whatever the decision, it will end in pure satisfaction. Walking through at any time of the year will bring its rewards, but the full picture comes into focus in spring and summer through the colours of the flowers and mature trees. There are plenty of information boards, well-maintained walkways, stone walls and trail markers for those preferring to abandon phone maps. Trickling streams, mini weirs, 'Billy Goats' Gruff' bridges – inviting Poohsticks races – and fairy steps, provide a natural playground. It is a great hideout for animals, and a common lizard is a recent addition to reported sightings.

The trail passes through the stunning Seven Arches Viaduct, Breary Marsh, the 'Slabbering Baby' water spout and remains of Scotland Mill's dam together with former tanneries. Well worth a visit is Hustler's Row, a group of 20 Yorkshire stone cottages built in 1871 for the quarry workers by their employer, John Husler (without the T).

When young, the writer Alan Bennett, whose father owned a local butcher's, often cycled through the trail on his way to deliver meat to the nearby home of the Fletcher family. Valerie Fletcher (1926–2012) later became the second wife of poet T. S. Eliot.

Address Start from Meanwood Park, Meanwood, Green Lane, LS6 4LE or Henry Marsden's statue, Woodhouse Moor, LS6 4LE | Getting there Meanwood Park: bus 51 or 52 to Green Road / Green View and Stainbeck Avenue; for Woodhouse Moor: bus 1, 5, 27, 28 or 56 to Hyde Park Road / Moorland Road; by car take the A 61 north of the city towards Woodhouse Moor and Meanwood beyond | Hours Accessible 24 hours | Tip The Three Cottages Café in Meanwood Park is open daily throughout the year, selling drinks and light meals to the trekkers and those just looking for refreshments in green spaces. There is plenty of outdoor seating suitable for dog owners.

68 Middleton Railway

The world's oldest continuously working railway

Who built the world's first steam locomotive? George Stephenson, perhaps? Wrong!

The answer and much more can be found in this lovely little museum and engine yard that sits on part of the oldest railway in the world, built in 1758. It is on the site of Middleton Broom, a coal pit where the whole story began. A small family of pit owners – the Brandlings – built the Middleton railway to get the coal into the centre of Leeds where it was most needed, but the trucks were pulled at the time, not by engines, but horses on wooden rails, which began to cost time and money.

John Blenkinsop, a mining engineer working for the Brandlings got together with respected Leeds engineer, Matthew Murray and jointly they designed and built Salamanca, the world's first steam locomotive. It is a remarkable story that this leap in engineering was aimed at solving a domestic dilemma.

To celebrate this piece of railway history, a group of local enthusiasts formed the Middleton Railway Trust Ltd in 1960, shortly before the pit officially closed in 1968. Their posse has expanded over the years to cement the railway's immortality and keep the memory alive. Visitors can view a preserved part of the oldest piece of stone railway anywhere in the world, sitting in a quiet corner of the museum, which relocated to its present site in 1996. You can view locomotives with endearing names such as Sweet Pea and Sir Berkeley, the latter of which featured in the classic film, *The Railway Children*. There are also the aptly titled Murray and Blenkinsop. A small shop and tea room are also present.

Sadly, Salamanca came to an untimely end six years after it was built when it suddenly exploded. Ironically, it was George Stephenson who reputedly gave evidence to an inquiry saying it was the fault of the driver who tampered with the boiler. Was the driver a member of the Luddites perhaps?

Address The Station, Moor Road, Hunslet, LS10 2JQ, +44 (0)845 680 1758, www.middletonrailway.org.uk | **Getting there** Bus 12, 13 or 13A to Belle Isle Road/Moor Road, Middleton; by car: leave the M 621 at Junction 5 or 6 depending on direction and follow signs for Hunslet, Beeston | **Hours** Diesel trains on Sat & Wed, steam trains Sun & bank holidays; first train departs from Moor Road at 11am. Check website for details of special trips. | **Tip** Get off at the end of the line at Park Halt and choose between the four trails for a walk in Middleton Park. Details can be found in the museum.

69 __ The Miners' Sculpture

A timeless reminder of a tragic past

'What did we learn? What should we learn?' wrote Ian McMillan, in his poem about the year-long Miners' Strike in 1984. The answer: 'quite a bit' comes to mind when walking through the former pit village of Allerton Bywater.

Situated on the edge of Leeds City Council's district, it has a shared cultural identity with nearby Castleford but carries a Wakefield postcode address – all clear signs that the community has a strong independent feel. Allerton Bywater now proudly exists as a forward-looking millennium village. It was selected for a sustainable housing programme, bringing solid award-winning businesses and a sense of purpose back to a place ripped apart by its pit closure.

On a corner of the village park, off Station Road, stands a striking sculpture designed and built by ex-miner, Harry Malkin. Modern housing and pit cottages form a fitting backdrop for the sculpture, which depicts a mining cage suspended by metal chains. Etched on its front are mine workers being carried into a perilous underground world: many never returned to the surface. Beside the rustic cage stand two coal trucks bearing the names of those who lost their lives while carrying out their job.

A Conservative government pit closure programme sparking the Miners' Strike, marked the beginning of the end for deep-coal mining in Britain. The last piece of coal was mined at Allerton in 1992, ending a 117-year history at a colliery scarred by tragedy, strikes, unemployment and fall-outs. During that time, an estimated 57.6 million tonnes of coal was mined, but the human cost was huge. Between 1875 and 1992, a total of 91 men and boys died working at Allerton Bywater Pit and 1,060 lost their jobs. Donations from relatives of those who died at Allerton partly met the cost of the £30,000 sculpture, which was unveiled in 2012 before marching brass bands and huge crowds from mining communities.

Address On the village park / green between Station Road and Robinson Road, WF 10 2DP |
Getting there Bus 167 or 168 to Castleford; by car: take the Selby Road out of Leeds and
follow signs for Garforth and Kippax before taking the B 6137 at Kippax towards Great
Preston / Allerton Bywater | **Hours** Accessible 24 hours | **Tip** Samuel and Valentine is a
lovely award-winning gourmet pie and cheese shop across the road from the sculpture on
Station Road. It is also a restaurant and takeaway and is available to hire as a party venue.

70 The Monks' Hiding Place

A chance to escape from Henry VIII

There is much to admire about the leafy village of Bardsey. Its residents can enjoy the comforts of quintessential English country living, blissfully aware that Leeds is 'nowt but' a hop, skip and a jump away to provide the income and a faster pace of life should they so wish.

At the heart of the village stands the Bingley Arms, thought to be the oldest pub in Britain, and with a birth date of 953 a.d., who could argue? To the left of the front entrance stands an Inglenook fireplace of great magnitude, and should the fire be unlit, customers are actively encouraged to immerse themselves in the grand entrance and look up to the chimney. There, they will find two priest holes, so named because 16th-century monks were often forced to make a hasty retreat from inevitable arrest and execution. They had to contort themselves into the small holes until the coast was clear.

The pub was known as The Priest's Inn until 1780, and once doubled up as a courthouse. It was a favourite watering hole for the monks on their way from Kirkstall Abbey in Leeds to St Mary's Abbey in York, but if caught wearing holy robes the consequences were dire. In 1536 and 1539, two suppression acts on the orders of Henry VIII aimed to abolish Catholic monasteries, convents and friaries and strip them of their wealth and religion. This move was intended to take away the papal power of Rome and place it into the hands of the Church of England of which Henry reigned supreme.

Yorkshire was a particular target for the king's men, as the Catholic clergy population was heavier in number and many defied orders to walk away from their faith. Locals colluded to shield the monks and a passageway leading to the nearby church was used as a second escape. Part of it still remains in the pub's cellar. Visitors wishing to have a small peek at the subterranean wonder may ask politely at the bar.

Address Church Lane, Bardsey, LS17 9DR, +44 (0)1937 572 462, www.bingleyarms.com | Getting there Bus X 98 or X 99 to Bardsey village; by car: take the A 58 from Leeds to Wetherby and turn off for the village of Bardsey | Hours Mon 4.30–10pm, Tue & Wed noon–11pm, Thu–Sat noon–midnight, Sun noon–1.30pm (food served for more restricted hours, so check website) | Tip All Hallows Church – the second monks' hideout – is another historic building in the village. Built in 950 a.d., it is thought to be one of the oldest surviving Anglo-Saxon churches in Britain. The clock is hand-wound, and inside the church is a lovely four-panelled tapestry that took local residents five years to create.

71 Morley Town Hall

The 'centre of the universe'

Writing about a return to her home town, young journalist Helen Fielding once made a tongue-in-cheek comment that Morley was 'the centre of the universe'. Fielding went on to become one of the world's most successful authors as the creator of *Bridget Jones's Diary*, and was quoting local businessman and cousin, Sir Harry Hardy.

Whether the late Sir Harry had uttered these exact words is a matter of conjecture, but he is just one of many Morleans immensely proud of their town, once independent from Leeds. Morley lies five miles to the west of the city and was built on seven hills. It can easily be identified on the Leeds skyline from the clock tower on its magnificent town hall, built between 1890 and 1895. The building was designed at a cost of £41,000 by George Fox, and stands at 160 feet (49 metres) high. The tower, which houses a Sam Rhodes clock, still provides a cultural magnet despite losing many of its civic services to Leeds in the late 1990s. The beautiful Alexandra Hall has been extensively used for dramas such as *Red Riding*, and the former magistrates' court room is often used for trial scenes in the soap opera *Emmerdale*. Many of the town hall's original features remain, including dining halls and former police cells, both viewable by appointment. The central staircase and stained-glass windows add to an overall picture of Victorian elegance. Local societies and clubs regularly meet there and concerts frequently take place inside Alexandra Hall.

Morley Town Hall has provided a backdrop for real-life political drama over the years. It was here in 2015 that former shadow Chancellor, Ed Balls, lost his Labour seat to Conservative, Andrea Jenkyns. In 1913, Morley-born Prime Minister, Herbert Asquith, returned to the town hall for an official visit. Never sympathetic to the suffragette cause, he was greeted by angry protestors who flung leaflets in his face.

Address 68 Queen Street, Morley, LS27 9DY, +44 (0)113 378 8575, www.leeds.gov.uk |
Getting there Bus 51 or 52 to Queen Street/Town Hall; by car: take the M 621 and
A 643 west from the city centre | Hours It is advisable to check the website, as a tour is
possible with a volunteer via the town clerk's office | Tip Information can be found in the
nearby shopping precinct for The Morley Heritage Trail. This is a potted history trail of
the town, which includes the lovely Scatcherd Park and tells the story of famous Morley
suffragette, Alice Scatcherd, as well as some of Morley's other famous residents.

72 Nellie's Tree

Ardour in the arboretum

Voted Britain's Best Tree by the Woodland Trust in 2019, this splendid beech started life as three separate saplings until a love-sick local decided to declare his undying ardour for his sweetheart 100 years ago. It stands in the heart of the Parlington Estate, once the seat of the Gascoigne family who came to this eastern part of Leeds from France in the 1700s.

Vic Stead – a miner from nearby Garforth – wandered dreamily through the Parlington Estate near Aberford each day on his way to work with thoughts of love for Nellie, a young dairymaid who had captured his heart. But, rather taciturn, Vic preferred to show rather than tell his darling. One day in 1920, spying the saplings standing handsomely in a row, Vic ingeniously decided to marry them together. This formed an N-shape for Nellie so that she would see his undying devotion when she too passed by.

Nellie's Tree – as it became known – has been a regional secret for many years, but local tree rescue campaigners, along with Vic's relative, Chris Lund, nominated it in the Woodland Trust's Best Tree competition launched on BBC's *The One Show*. To their delight, it was indeed voted the UK's best in 2019, beating a giant redwood into second place and even came 9th in the European Tree of the Year competition. Now a proper giant in the woods, it is also known as the 'love tree', and Vic's actions have inspired many subsequent proposals over the intervening years. Nellie's Tree has made heroes of the pair.

But did all this wooing in the woodland actually work out for Vic and Nellie? Indeed it did, as the couple married and have a living grandson – none other than Chris Lund, who proudly views it as a fitting tribute to the couple! According to those in the know, they remained happily married until their passing, but their dedication to one another is now etched for many years to come in a ferny forest floor.

Address Parlington Estate, LS25 3EH | Getting there Bus 64 to Cattle Lane, Barwick Lodge, then it is 30-minute walk from there; by car: head out of the city on the A 64 York Road to Barwick-in-Elmet before taking Potterton Lane, then Long Lane. Nellie's Tree is off Long Lane on the left, | Hours Accessible 24 hours | Tip In the nearby village of Aberford are the Gascoigne Almshouses, designed by George Fowler Jones and built in 1844 at the behest of Isabella and Elizabeth Gascoigne. The alms houses were built to house the poor as the sisters' tribute to their father and brothers Richard and Thomas in the wake of their deaths.

73___ The New Penny

A trailblazer for LGBTQIA venues

Britain's cities in the 1960s and 1970s could be violent places, where racial and homophobic attacks happened on a frequent basis. The New Penny pub in Leeds provided one of the country's first safe havens for the gay community, and is still popular with the LGBTQIA fraternity today.

The pub – in the heart of The Calls district – started out as The Hope and Anchor in 1953, welcoming a covert gay community who wanted to socialise away from prying, prejudiced eyes at a time when homosexuality was illegal. It was a bold move to open the pub, as its arrival to the city happened four years before the publication of The Wolfenden Report that suggested new laws should be enforced to protect the rights of the gay community. Those recommendations led to the 1967 Sexual Offences Act, a decade after the recommendations were made. One year later, The Hope and Anchor was attacked by certain homophobic groups of football fans who, after a Leeds United v Glasgow Rangers match at Elland Road, went on a rampage, attacking the pub, causing substantial damage and forcing its temporary closure. It was thought at the time that the identity of the pub had been leaked in a national newspaper article, sparking the riot.

The Hope and Anchor became The New Penny in 1975 and is now the country's longest continually running venue for LGBTQIA customers. However, its owners stress that The New Penny is open to absolutely everyone and holds no prejudices. Its late night licence has meant a substantial customer base, some opting to travel from all over the UK as closing times at 4.30am and 5.30am have allowed them the luxury of catching the early morning trains back home. The pub has disc-spinning drag queens such as Sordid Secret on a regular basis, but past acts have included Lily Savage and Amber Dextrous. Staff support the annual Leeds Pride parade, held on the first Sunday in August.

Address 57–59 The Calls, LS1 7BT, +44 (0)113 243 8055, Facebook: @TheNewPennyLeeds | Getting there Bus 117, 118, 118A, 118S or X17 to Call Lane | Hours Mon–Thu 8pm–4am, Fri 8pm–5.30am, Sat noon–5.30am, Sun noon–3am | Tip Mill Hill Unitarian Church on the corner of City Square / Park Row was the first place of worship in Leeds to conduct same-sex couple ceremonies after they were made legal in 2014.

74 Nicola Adams
Golden Post Box

Celebrating the eternal sunshine of a local hero

Such golden landmarks are not handed out lightly, and Leeds has a rich list of sporting heroes from which to cherry pick. Two in particular caught the attention of the Royal Mail.

One of the chosen ones is a slight, cherubic-faced boxer with buckets of talent and nerve, and two double golden pillar boxes stand proudly in her honour on Cookridge Street, matching her double Olympic titles.

Leeds lass Nicola Adams made history after becoming an Olympic flyweight champion in the London 2012 and Rio 2016 games. Nicola also played her part in a huge milestone for live television: She was one half of the first ever, same sex couple to take to the floor on BBC's Strictly Come Dancing in 2020. But it was by sheer chance that the former pupil of Agnes Stewart School in Leeds began boxing when she was taken to a local club by mum, Dee, lacking a babysitter for her young daughter that day. She supplemented her boxing expenses with extra work on television, as this particular women's sport was not funded in her early days. Nicola became an MBE in 2013 and was awarded an Honorary Doctor of Laws degree by the University of Leeds. She is also a campaigner for LGBTQIA rights and an avid supporter of causes in the city she has refused to abandon.

But which other golden Leeds athlete has been given a similar accolade? Olympic and World champion triathlete Alistair Brownlee has a golden post box in his honour in Horsforth, north of the city. Both athletes will soon be looking beyond sporting success, but since retiring Nicola has admitted she wouldn't mind doing a spot of acting. It's not difficult to imagine her swapping the silence of the extra for lines such as 'We've been expecting you Mr Bond!'

LIFT ACCESS
THIS WAY

Address On the corner of Cookridge Street and The Headrow close to Leeds Art Gallery in the city centre | Getting there Bus 27, 28 or 49 to Calverley Street | Hours Accessible 24 hours | Tip Alistair Brownlee's official golden post box (an unofficial one was painted in his home village of Bramhope) is in the suburban town of Horsforth outside the post office at New Road Side, Horsforth.

75_Oddball

Odd-looking but a real trooper

Oddball is a retired giant excavator presiding over the rolling pastures of St Aidan's Nature Reserve at Swillington. It remains the largest preserved walking dragline in Western Europe and is a unique visitor attraction.

It was saved from the scrap heap more than 20 years ago, thanks to Friends of St Aidan's, a group of volunteers who successfully persuaded mining boss, the late Richard Budge, to donate it to the public. Oddball now sits permanently on terra firma, and the friends and trustees organise open days three times a year to welcome visitors and impart sound knowledge. Originally named Clinchfield, this Bucyrus dragline was made in the US in 1948 and took the journey across the Atlantic in the 1950s to help Britain's clean-up after World War II. The 1,200-tonne machine settled at St Aidan's in 1974 to accompany Big Bob – another dragline – with both acting as giant scoops to transport the coal from the ground. Opencast workers, nicknamed 'Sunshine Miners' due to their tasks above ground, coined the nickname 'Oddball' because of the initial differences to its electricity supply, compared with the more mainstream Bob. It also made strange noises while going about its daily work so was deemed a bit of a misfit. Draglines were the brainchild of John Page who invented the first one in 1904 for work on the Chicago Canal. The first walking dragline with feet or pontoons, was built in 1923 to minimise heavy pressure, a feat that caterpillar tracks were unable to achieve. They were huge machines, some standing 22-storeys high. Sadly, Oddball was unable to carry on after a terrible flood at St Aidan's in 1988 deemed it inoperable. Big Bob continued to fight a lone battle at St Aidan's but 'died' in 1998 after he was sold for scrap metal when opencast mining finally ceased in 1998. Oddball is also a permanent tribute to the Sunshine Miners.

Address Astley Lane, Swillington, LS26 8AL, www.walkingdragline.org | Getting there
Bus 167 or 168 to Swillington; by car: take the A642 through the villages of Oulton and
Woodlesford before reaching Swillington | Hours Open days are usually held in the spring,
summer and early autumn months, 1–4pm, but dates vary each year so it is advisable to
check the website | Tip St Aidan's Nature Park at Astley Lane, opened in 2002, following
the closure of opencast mining in the area. It is a fantastic place to visit all year round, with
more than 100 types of birds and a wide variety of fauna and flora.

76 The Old Bear Pit

Gateway to a place that time forgot

This is an impressive little landmark with an identity crisis, standing almost forlornly on Headingley's Cardigan Road. It is often ignored, taken for granted but sometimes remembered with fondness by locals.

The Old Bear Pit, a Grade II-listed building, was the gateway to Leeds' only Zoological and Botanical Gardens to date. It is so named as the bears, considered the star attractions in the zoo, could be observed from above via the gateway's two castellated turrets. They bookend the brick entrance gate which, with its three arches, takes on an almost medieval appearance.

The gardens opened in 1840, courtesy of the local council, and were considered a welcome retreat away from the suffocating industrial soot-laden air of central Leeds. Children especially loved climbing the stone steps inside the tiny turrets to view the bears in a circular pit. Residents thought they never had it so good strolling among the exotic trees and plants while enjoying the animals.

The entrance fee of 6d (old pence) for adults and 3d for children was considered pricey in those days, even for relatively affluent nearby residents. This, together with the added complication of the small weekend window of opening times, led to its closure in 1848. It was sold to a local entrepreneur who in turn made financial gains by relinquishing plots of the land.

The acreage of the old gardens beyond the Bear Pit has shrunk somewhat, giving way to various housing developments over the years, but a sizeable plot, threadbare and barren, still stands. Leeds Civic Trust took the Bear Pit on and restored the brick building in the 1960s; it is still under the trust's ownership to this day and members say plans are afoot to improve the area around it. Keeping animals in such a confined enclosure is, today, rightly questionable, but the hope is that this little landmark might be loved again one day.

Address 53 Cardigan Road, Headingley, LS6 3DN | **Getting there** Bus 19 or 19A to Cardigan Road or 56 to Cardigan Road/Victoria Road; by car: head north on Kirkstall Road/A65 towards Cardigan Road | **Hours** Accessible 24 hours | **Tip** Just a short walk away, on Weetwood Lane, is a little gem of a park called The Hollies that contains beautiful plants, trees and lovely walkways.

77 Opera North
Not just for the privileged few

The world of opera, with its libretti, arias, mezzo-sopranos and tenors, might seem to belong to a rather imperious world, strangely detached from the no-nonsense folk of Yorkshire. But Opera North has brought informality and accessibility to this genre since its arrival in Leeds 43 years ago.

The company broke from the traditional shackles of London's Royal Opera House in Covent Garden and by doing so its intention was to take the genre north, and dispel some misconceptions that opera was only for the snooty world of the Southern élite. Most of the performances take place in the dual purpose, Grand Theatre and Opera House – built in 1878 – but the company regularly heads out on the road to Salford, Newcastle and Nottingham. The more traditional operas such as Puccini's *La Bohème* or Wagner's *Ring Cycle* take to the stage, but the annual programme is rich and varied, and contemporary performances such as *Street Scene* and *The Greek Passion* can also be enjoyed. Many of the operas are sung in English, but there are surtitles if performed in Italian, German or French.

Opera North has recently been given a Theatre of Sanctuary Status, a recognition for its work with refugees and asylum seekers in the city, and has reached out to more than 100 communities with workshops, discussions and performances. Each year, six community groups in the region are chosen to embark on a collaborative programme of cultural events with the company. Choirs for young and old and lunchtime impromptu concerts, all add to the strong message that this is for everyone and not just a few. Ticket prices are kept deliberately low, especially for 16- to 29-year-olds to avoid closing the door to students and those on low incomes. New rehearsal and performance spaces will soon be housed in the Howard Assembly Room and Howard Opera Centre, which was ready for the curtain call in 2021.

Address Opera North, Grand Theatre, 46 New Briggate, LS1 6NU, +44 (0)113 223 3600, www.operanorth.co.uk | Getting there Bus 2, 3, 3A, 7, 11, X 98 or X 99 to New Briggate | Hours Telephone or check website for performance times | Tip Phoenix Dance Theatre was created in the city by three young Black men from Harehills: Donald Edwards, David Hamilton and Vilmore Jones. From domestic performances, the company grew to become a touring company that now performs regularly in a space shared with Northern Ballet at Quarry Hill, Leeds.

78   The ORT School
Provided a 'passport to life' for refugees

The ORT School only had a short tenure in Leeds, but it had a life-long impact on 106 Jewish teenagers and their teachers, who cheated almost certain death at the hands of the Nazis during World War II. The boys had fled their ORT school in East Berlin, just days before the outbreak of the war as anti-Semitism was already on the rise. The boys were the first group chosen to accompany seven teachers and their wives, and the remaining ORT pupils were to follow on a few days later. War was declared on 1 September, and the other 109 boys were not so lucky: most of them died in the death camps.

The escapees were initially shielded in a Kitchener-run camp in Kent and were greeted by locals who threw sweets and chocolates their way. They headed north and settled in hostels in and around Chapeltown Road. The ORT Technical Engineering School in Roseville Avenue was to be their seat of learning from 1940 until 1942. The temporary school was set up in haste by British ORT officials, Colonel Joseph Levey and Dr Simon Walker, who had managed to convince the German authorities that the school already existed. The boys were brought to Leeds as it already housed a well-established Jewish community. The teenagers, aged between 15 and 17 were taught trades in keeping with the ORT tradition.

The idea for the ORT schools originated in the Russian city of St Petersburg in 1880 to help impoverished Jews, held back by the weight of persecution by the pogroms, but the idea was adopted by other countries, including Britain. The name ORT is a Russian acronym which, translated, means 'Society for Trades and Agricultural Labour'. Many of the Leeds old ORT boys stayed in the city, and eight of them reunited to mark the 70th anniversary of the Roseville Avenue school in 2010. The site of the ORT hostel for the boys, since 2013 marked by a blue plaque, is now a Muslim school for girls.

Address Newton Hill, Chapeltown Road, LS7 4JE | Getting there Bus 2, 3, 3A or 36 to Newton Hill Road/Chapeltown Road | Hours Accessible 24 hours | Tip The Polish Centre at Newton Hill was also established by immigrants who formed their own club after World War II to keep the Polish language and traditions alive. They hold cultural events at the centre.

79 Otley Chevin

A surprise round every corner

Should a 'southerner' ever use insulting words with 'up', 'north', 'grim' and 'it's', you may be forgiven for climbing up to the top of the nearest peak and letting out the most enormous scream you can muster. What better high ground to vent your anger than Surprise View at Otley Chevin that offers the most privileged of views over Wharfedale?

The word 'chevin' is thought to have derived from the Brythonic word (Welsh Celtic) 'cefyn', meaning 'a ridge of high ground', and the summit at Surprise View reaches a peak of 925 feet (282 metres). It provides panoramic views over North Yorkshire with Otley nestling nicely in the valley below, and these views are said to have inspired Turner's painting *Snow Storm: Hannibal and His Army Crossing the Alps*. The millstone grit rock on the top is thought to have been formed 300 million years ago and it is well served by footpaths and bridleways.

The chevin is still a favourite with artists as well as sporty types who take part in orienteering and bouldering. Pride of place at the chevin each Easter is the 36 foot (11 metre) cross that is carefully sited two weeks before the festival and dismantled a fortnight later. The move was a symbol of unity between different denominations of Otley Council of Christian Churches. Reuniting the cross with the chevin requires military precision by locals who march the cross to the top of the hill and hoist it in place. This ritual began in 1968, and during this inaugural year an 'act of God' blew over the cross following a night of strong gales. The original cross had to be replaced due to vandalism and wear and tear. Craftsman Brett Thompson used reclaimed timber from Manchester's Arndale Centre, which was obliterated in the 1996 IRA bombing. The new cross was a symbolic prayer for peace and rebirth and this came two years before the Northern Ireland Peace Agreement was announced.

Address Otley Chevin, Otley, LS21 3JL | Getting there Bus X 84 to Russell Farm and a 30-minute walk; by car: take the A 660, Otley Road from Leeds and turn left into York Gate | Hours Accessible 24 hours | Tip Far from being a race for those sporty types, the famous – or infamous – Otley Run is a pub crawl race, as Otley boasts 20 pubs – a lot for a town of its size! The 'run' is a favourite with students, stag and hen parties or those simply wanting a top night out.

80_ The Otters of Leeds

'Lutra Lutra' loves Leeds

You could be forgiven for thinking Leeds city centre a highly unlikely place to do a spot of otter watching. O ye of little faith.

Leeds first made wildlife headlines in 2002 when a keen-eyed security guard captured an otter taking a swim under the Dark Arches, and since then there have been several sightings up and down the water banks of the city centre. Sylvia Jay, an Otley-based ecologist, confirmed that footprints and otter droppings, known as spraints, have been discovered recently on the banks near to the Dark Arches close to the city's railway station.

It is a quite remarkable comeback for Britain's native Eurasian otters, which were teetering on the brink of extinction for most of the 20th century where numbers saw a 95 per cent decline. The mass clean-up of waterways and the recent withdrawal of organochlorine chemicals have now encouraged numbers to rise by more than 55 per cent.

The otters – also known as Lutra Lutra – are part of the Mustelid family and are famous for being pathologically shy creatures, so keen spotters need untold patience if they are to glimpse them in Leeds. You are most likely to encounter an otter very early at dawn or late at night down by the water's edge. They love sloping river banks and sheltered vegetation and mostly feed on fish and insects, though small mammals and birds are not exempt from the otter's menu. Their solitary lifestyle also means they are, more often than not, alone so it's unlikely you would happen upon a family.

They are a protected species but are not always on everyone's list of favourites, especially with some keen anglers, but their sheer elegance and their dedicated work ethic mesmerise the vast majority of wildlife enthusiasts. Those proposing to spot an otter should look out for webbed toe prints in the mud, spraints and the faint aroma of Jasmin tea, which apparently has been likened to their scent!

Address Dark Neville Street, under the railway tunnels, LS1 4GS | **Getting there** Head
to the city's railway station using the South Entrance Exit (see ch. 93) | **Hours** Accessible
24 hours | **Tip** The Hop, also on Dark Neville Street, is run by local Ossett brewery selling
a fine selection of local beers and gourmet pies, and there are regular live gigs.

81 Pompocali
What did the Romans ever do for Thorner?

The Romans seemed to be quite fond of Yorkshire: we can see this on our travels in ancient settlements throughout the great county. Some historians lament that the incessant modernisation of Leeds has deprived the city of some ancient fortified sites, believed to have once stood on hallowed ground in the city.

Perhaps this is why a pleasant pocket of wood and grassland, close to the rural villages of Thorner and Bardsey, is known as Pompocali. The Romanesque name, given by locals, seems to have stuck over the years after speculation first mounted over the identity of two curious horseshoe-shaped mounds. Residents – Thorner lays claim over Bardsey – thought it was the site of a Roman fort, as it lies in close proximity to a credited Roman road near to the village and to an ancient quarry. Could this have provided the stone the Romans needed to build a road taking them northwards?

However, after careful archaeological research, experts declared that, on the balance of probability, the scales were more likely to be tipped in favour of this being an ancient spoil heap and not a Roman fort. Solace can be sought from the fact that this, and close neighbour Norwood Bottoms (not a person) was designated a Site of Special Scientific Interest – no small achievement, and it still attracts attention from 'believers' along with the curious, who remain forever loyal to the historical place.

It is a short and pleasant walk from Pompocali into Thorner, which is in turn an ancient village, listed in the Domesday Book in 1086. A medieval market cross can be found here, and St Osyth's Well, close to St Peter's Church, is located in Sam Syke Ginnel, a local name for 'passageway'. The country lanes provide access to the only example of magnesium limestone woodland, and Thorner is known for being one of a cluster of 'dark villages' devoid of street lighting: the residents prefer it this way.

Address Milner Lane, LS14 3AQ, www.thornerhistory.org.uk | Getting there Bus 7 to Thorner village. The walk is suited to those who enjoy a bit of a trek. Follow the old Roman road, marked, from the village, crossing over the beck and heading north where the earthworks are signed; by car: follow the Wetherby Road (A 58) from the city centre and turn left at East Rigton down Home Farm Lane and into Milner Lane | Hours Accessible 24 hours | Tip The villages of Thorner and Bardsey cum Rigton are filled with historical, listed buildings such as 16th and 17th century barns, farmhouses and cottages. Check out Sam Sykes Ginnel in Church View where you can find St Osyth's Well just west of the church. St Osyth was believed to be a Viking saint.

82 Post Hill

A huff and a puff will get you up to the top

Post Hill is one of those little pockets of charming hideaways that are so rudely overlooked by city slickers. Perhaps the locals prefer it that way. It should, though, be given a deserving seat at the dinner table of delights in Leeds.

Covering more than 28 acres between Farnley and Pudsey becks, Post Hill is a little beauty spot used by running clubs, dog walkers and nature lovers, and has slowly reverted to its natural state after a chequered past. During the 1920s, it was the prime site in the city for motorcycle scrambling. It was used as an internment camp during World War II for German and Italian prisoners of war, who were put to work cultivating the land. Later the local *Yorkshire Post* newspaper acquired the land and gave it the name that it still answers to today.

The hill peaks at just over 410 feet (125 metres) and was once ideal for daring scramblers. It was coined 'the steepest freak climb in the world'. Crowds flocked each weekend to watch daredevil stunts but an accident in 1931, during a race, led to the death of a spectator, sparking safety concerns. The tragedy was caused by an overturned tractor, and bikers thought it unfair to jump to knee-jerk reactions and blame them; nevertheless, racing came to an end. Scramblers are still forbidden on the site today but West Leeds Motor Club organises ad-hoc bike trials, so it hasn't entirely disappeared. Pudsey runners huff and puff up the steep grassy bank on occasions, and the famous Pudsey 5k run takes place at Post Hill.

The site is cared for by Fields in Trust and Leeds Parks and Countryside and you can take a walk through the acid grasslands and ancient woodland that has trees dating back to the 1600s. Roe deer, tawny owls and rare breeds of bat are just some of the wildlife sheltering and hunting here. A hike trail circumnavigates the green oasis that triggers a rural unity between Farnley and Pudsey.

Address Pudsey Road/Wood Lane, LS12 5ST, +44 (0)113 232 9973, www.leeds.gov.uk |
Getting there Bus 4, 4G, 80, 81 or 81A to Pudsey Road; by car: Post Hill lies off the Ring
Road (A 6110) between Pudsey and Farnley and a small car park is provided on Wood
Lane | Hours Accessible 24 hours, but advisable to check the website for parking time
restrictions | Tip Farnley Hall Fishpond Nature Reserve at Farnley Hall is a new kid on the
block to Leeds' little green secrets, only becoming a nature reserve in 2004, but it is full of
interesting flora and fauna.

83 Potternewton Park

Where two-tone became one with anti-racism

This pretty park in the middle of multicultural Chapeltown becomes a colourful spectacle once a year when the Leeds West Indian Carnival starts its glorious way from Potternewton before snaking the streets of LS 7.

The carnival isn't the only event in Potternewton's list of historical claims to fame. It provided the backdrop for one of the final and highest profile political concerts in the history of popular culture, headlined by The Specials. A Rock Against Racism and Anti-Nazi League concert took place at Potternewton on a summer's day in 1981, coinciding with a one-off sister carnival against racism. This was fuelled by civil unrest and riots throughout Britain's towns and cities and organisers wanted to spread a message that a culture of tolerance should triumph over racial inequality. The Rock Against Racism movement began in 1976 with backing from bands like The Clash and the Tom Robinson Band playing concerts to raise awareness of rising nationalism.

Many thought Leeds was a fitting final resting place to bring the curtain down on a series of similar concerts held nationally over five years. Thoughts were never far away from David Oluwale, a British Nigerian homeless man who was found dead in the River Aire in Leeds 12 years earlier. Foul play brought on by racial prejudice was thought to be the motive and fingers were firmly pointed at the city's police force.

The Specials headlined the Leeds concert, which was organised largely by the local RAR group. They were part of a group of two-tone bands named after their record label and included groups such as The Selecter, The Beat and The Mob. The bands were usually made up of multiracial members who performed ska and reggae music. The Leeds concert, which also featured Aswad, Misty in Roots along with local bands The Mekons and Gang of Four, was hailed a huge success in the fight against racism.

Address Potternewton Park, Chapeltown, LS7 4HB | Getting there Bus 2, 3 or 3A to
Chapeltown Road | Hours Accessible 24 hours; carnival takes place over the August bank
holiday weekend | Tip Roundhay Park nearby is a good way to spend an afternoon with
its butterfly and tropical gardens but did you know it was the site of the first-ever powered
flight by Robert Blackburn? The park was used as an airfield for Blackburn to test fly his
monoplane in 1909.

84 Quebecs Hotel

Swapping Herbert Asquith for Helena Bonham Carter

The Liberals were once the dominant political party in Leeds during the 19th and early 20th centuries, which led them to indulge lavishly in their popularity by opening their very own club. This has been lovingly restored to its former glory, reincarnated now as Quebecs Hotel.

The grand Leeds & County Liberal Club opened in 1891 with the laying of the final stone carried out by Sir James Kitson, a prominent Liberal MP from Leeds and later 1st Baron of Airedale. More than 1,600 would-be members (women were excluded) formed an orderly queue to join, paying an annual sum of three guineas in old British currency.

The club – which was built with a Welsh terracotta clay – welcomed such prominent guests in its lifetime as Morley-born Herbert Asquith, Britain's Liberal Prime Minister from 1908 to 1916. However, falling party membership forced the club's closure after World War II.

Haughty heckles are now a distant memory and have been replaced with the chatter of guests such as Asquith's own great-granddaughter, Helena Bonham Carter. The actor is just one of many famous faces to have stayed at Quebecs, including Lady Gaga, Pharrell Williams and Bill Nighy. The hotel – which opened in 2002 – offers them a spot of luxury, as it was painstakingly renovated back to its old self. The original cornice ceilings were hideously hidden by polystyrene when it served as offices in the 1970s and 1980s.

Quebecs is a Grade II-listed, four-star hotel with 44 splendid rooms. It has a sweeping original grand oak staircase, Corinthian columns and Renaissance carvings. During their stay, Caroline, Quebecs' affable manager, gently invites guests to carry out a spot of quizzing about the magnificent original stained-glass window. It is a centrepiece on the main stairway and is illustrated with the coats of arms of prominent Yorkshire towns written in old English. The trick is to guess the town!

Address 9 Quebec Street, LS1 2HA, +44 (0)113 244 8989, www.QuebecsHotel.co.uk |
Getting there 1-minute walk from Leeds Railway Station to the other side of City Square |
Hours Unrestricted to guests | Tip The Leeds Met (formerly the Metropolitan Hotel) is
just around the corner in King Street and is another example of a red fired terracotta clay
building. This was sourced locally in Burmantofts terracotta clay.

85 — The Rhubarb Triangle

Just waiting for a bit of custard

Why did an odd-looking vegetable plant growing on the banks of the Volga become synonymous with a geometrical slice of 'God's Own Country'? West Yorkshire's 'Rhubarb Triangle' – an area between Morley, Leeds and Wakefield – still remains one of the world's largest producers of the vegetable. Contrary to popular belief, rhubarb IS a vegetable and not a fruit and is recognised as much more than a stodgy pie filling. It was first spotted growing in Yorkshire during the 1600s. So why here? Water, nitrogen and cold weather are three explanations. The triangle nestles in a frost pocket of the nearby Pennines and the soil is rich in nitrogen due to the 'shoddy' and 'mungo' waste from the local woollen mills. The composition of Yorkshire water is also particularly attractive to the plant. Yorkshire once even had its own specially titled rhubarb express trains taking the produce swiftly to many UK fruit and vegetable markets.

Rhubarb is taken from the fields and cultivated in dimly lit sheds by candlelight to become forced rhubarb. The absence of photosynthesis in the growing means it becomes a sweeter version of itself and can be sold out of season. Today, the Rhubarb Triangle is to Yorkshire what the pasty is to Cornwall and has now joined a list of protected food names courtesy of the European Union.

One family of farmers has been a major player in rhubarb for five generations. The Oldroyds open their sheds in Rothwell to the public from January to March and some travel from all corners of the globe to take a sneaky peak and watch the picking of the pretty pink phosphorescent sticks.

Fourth-generation grower, Janet Oldroyd Hulme, and her family are spotted selling their wares with alacrity every year in February at the Wakefield Rhubarb Festival. They are known in farming circles as rhubarb royalty, and Janet's title? The 'High Priestess of Rhubarb'.

Address Ashfield Farm, Main Street, Carlton, WF3 3RW, +44 (0)133 2822245,
www.yorkshirerhubarb.co.uk | Getting there Bus 443 to Carlton Cricket Club; by car:
M62 then exit at J30 and follow the signpost for Wakefield and then for the village of
Carlton | Hours Pre-booked visits only – visit website for booking form | Tip The Triangle
Shop at nearby Dobson's Farm, Ouzlewell Green, has been in the family since 1815. Open
daily, you can purchase rhubarb treats and other tasty produce.

86__Rob Burrow Mural
A fitting dedication to a local hero

The moment when Kevin Sinfield picked up his best pal Rob Burrow from his wheelchair and carefully carried him over the finish line of the Leeds Marathon epitomised the enduring power of true friendship. Teammates at Leeds Rhinos Rugby League Club for many years, the two local heroes completed the inaugural Rob Burrow 2023 Leeds Marathon together, closely followed by Rob's devoted wife Lindsey. They have raised millions of pounds for Motor Neurone Disease (MND) research since Rob's diagnosis in 2019.

Sinfield played loose forward with the Rhinos and had previously completed seven marathons in seven days, raising over £2 million and helping create a research project for the Motor Neurone Disease Appeal. He has been awarded an OBE, and he has kept his promise to carry on fundraising for the cause until a cure is found. He has completed many more runs, including a 101-mile marathon from the Leicester Tigers' ground to his beloved Rhinos' Headingley Stadium.

To acknowledge the pair's strength and bravery and to raise awareness of this currently incurable illness that affects the brain and nerves, the Leeds Rhinos, Leeds City Council and the BBC unanimously agreed to commission a mural dedicated to Rob Burrow. The mural, painted by street artist 'Akse' on a background created by Kieran Hadley, was unveiled on the wall of Leeds Beckett University's Student Union in 2020. It is a portrait of Rob dressed in his Leeds number 7 kit during his heyday with the Rhinos, when he played scrum half. He made 493 appearances for his club and won eight Super League Championships, as well as three World Club Challenge trophies and a trio of League Leaders Shields.

Rob, who was also capped 20 times for England and the Great Britain team, wrote an inspirational message for the mural, which reads, 'In a world full of adversity, we must dare to dream.'

Address Leeds Beckett University City Campus, Woodhouse Lane, LS1 3HE | Getting there Bus 1 from Leeds Railway Station and buses 6, 8, 27, 28 and 85 from Leeds Bus Station, Albion Street or St John Centre | Hours Unrestricted | Tip At Leeds Beckett University you will find Broadcasting Tower, also known as the Rusty Building as it is built from COR-TEN weathering steel giving it a rusty appearance. It resembles a 70-metre (230-foot) high disorganised stack of boxes and accommodates Leeds Beckett University students. In 2010, it was named the Best Tall Building in the World by the Council for Tall Buildings and Urban Habitat.

87 Rodley Nature Reserve

A natural wonder in the heart of urbanity

Head west from Leeds centre and you will find, sandwiched in an urban basin, this splendid natural wonder of a place.

Rodley Nature Reserve stands on what was a Yorkshire Water sewage works up until 20 years ago, and now provides a sweeter smelling gorgeous picture in an urban brick house frame. The old pumping station is the only reminder of its utilitarian past. When the land was finally vacated, eagle-eyed locals saw its potential and persuaded the owners to lease a slice of it to transform this ugly duckling into a magnificent swan.

The nature park – run entirely by fundraising volunteers – opened to the public in 2000. BBC *Countryfile* magazine recognised it recently as one of the best independent reserves in the UK. Its accommodating accessibility, for those living with disabilities, has also been nationally applauded.

It includes a lagoon, the John Ackroyd Flower Meadow – in memory of one of the reserve's original trustees – a huge coppice, dragonfly ponds, visitor centre, a manager's garden, bird hides, viewpoints and a little café. Much of the food is lovingly made by volunteers who also serve the teas, maintain the grounds and care for the flora and fauna, to name but a few of the tasks required on a daily basis.

Rodley boasts its very own pass that allows migratory fish, such as salmon and brown trout, to traverse with ease the high weir on the River Aire that runs through the reserve. It is also a magnet to keen 'birders' who visit in droves, armed with long lenses and sandwiches, longing to spot the rich bird life. There has been a rare sighting of a white Tailed Eagle, captured on camera along with another urban rarity, the otter. Harvest mice numbers have successfully risen on the reserve, and foxes, weasels, shrews, bank voles and the comeback kid of rodents, the water vole, are regularly seen.

Address Moss Bridge Road, Rodley, LS13 1HP +44 (0)113 204 0441, www.rodleynaturereserve.org | Getting there Bus 35 or 60 to Rodley Town Street; by car: take the A 6120 Leeds Ring Road then follow the brown signs when turning onto the A 657 | Hours Mar–Oct 9am–5pm, Nov–Feb 9am–4pm on Wed, Sat, Sun & most bank holidays | Tip If you walk along the Leeds Liverpool Canal – also running through the reserve at Rodley – head towards Calverley and you will find The Tiny Tea Room at Calverley Bridge. This offers great home-made food and delicious cakes.

88 The Silver Cross Pram

A favourite of Her Majesty

In 1977, Princess Anne was presented with the gift of an iconic Silver Cross pram to welcome the arrival of her first child, Peter. The baby carriage is still a long-held favourite of the Royals and Her Late Majesty Queen Elizabeth II was often pictured pushing her babies around palace gardens. More recently, the Duke and Duchess of Cambridge were spotted out and about with one. However, the pram's embryonic roots started in a working-class district of Leeds.

An original Silver Cross pram from the mid-20th century can be found on display at Leeds Discovery Centre, a purpose-built Aladdin's cave of a place, housing thousands of museum pieces and artefacts. The pram was the brainchild of Leeds engineer William Wilson, who invented this particular perambulator – to give it its elongated name – in 1877. Wilson began trading from his factory in Silver Cross Street in industrial Hunslet, lying close to the city centre. Its unique selling point was not only its pleasing appearance, but Wilson developed a sophisticated spring system for a more efficient mobility and added a reversible hood. Business was soon booming and Silver Cross moved to larger premises in the more affluent village of Guiseley during the 1930s. Later, his three sons carried on with the growing business, which was known as the Rolls-Royce of prams, even featuring in the film *Mary Poppins*. Demand was high and around 35,000 were produced annually to meet worldwide orders. The Silver Cross name expanded to include buggies, car seats and other nursery products.

The Guiseley factory closed in 2002 due to a crowded market and a depleted workforce but the brand continues under the ownership of the Halsall company, which still operates a Yorkshire factory in Skipton as well as globally. Following its closure, hundreds gathered in Guiseley for an auction of factory memorabilia in an attempt to keep the Leeds link alive.

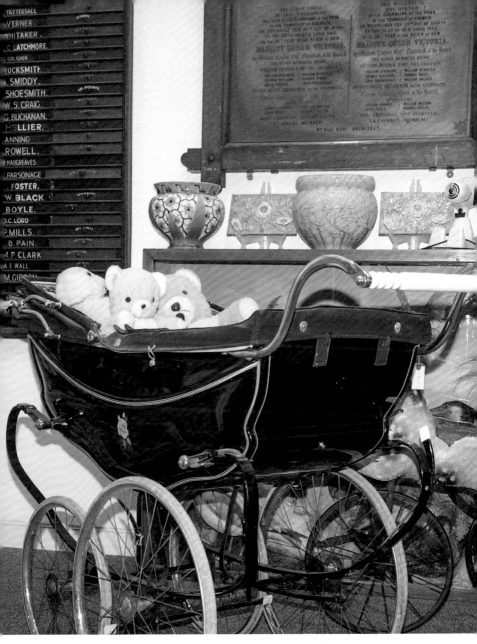

Address Leeds Discovery Centre, Carlisle Road, LS10 1LB, +44 (0)113 378 2100, www.museumsandgalleries.leeds.gov.uk/leeds-discovery-centre | Getting there Bus 28 to Clarence Road, Liberty Dock | Hours Thu 11am–2pm, or by appointment on other days | Tip Leeds Discovery Centre staff also work with schools and communities and hold regular tours of their stored items. There is also a community space that can be privately hired next to the temperature-regulated storage warehouse.

89 The Six Dales Trail
The route that keeps on giving

You'd be hard pushed to ramble in countryside more breathtaking than the stunning Yorkshire Dales, and one particular trail lies close to the centre of Leeds.

The Six Dales Trail is a long-distance footpath that begins in the market town of Otley on the outskirts of Leeds, before traversing the county line from West to North Yorkshire and finishing in the Yorkshire Dales National Park in the charming town of Middleham. The 38-mile (61-kilometre) trail was opened in 2010 by broadcaster and journalist, Janet Street-Porter, a keen walker herself who divides her time between her native London and adopted North Yorkshire. The hike is the brainchild of the Walkers Are Welcome group of Otley, who give their time to uncover new routes and highlight established ones, thus promoting the joys of rambling. Improvements to mental and physical health, as well as the environment, are firm benefits of this particular outdoor pursuit, and the group is dedicated to spreading the word.

Members have kindly organised the walk to form a game of two halves, giving a helping hand to novice walkers hoping to tackle the route. The first section of the trail takes off from Otley and heads for the market town of Pateley Bridge before merging into the second half of the journey to Middleham, famous for its 12th-century castle, once the home of Richard III. As its name suggests, the footpath lovingly meanders through six dales: Wharfedale, Washburndale, Nidderdale, Colsterdale, Coverdale and Wensleydale. The word 'dale' is an old Norse phrase meaning valley.

Rich rewards lie in wait for the pilgrims along the way, including a walk around four reservoirs, quaint villages, woods, rivers, ascents and descents. The 12th-century Jervaulx Abbey is another star attraction. The view simply keeps on giving to the finish in Wensleydale; or could it be the start depending on your preferred direction?

Address Start at Otley Buttercross, LS21 1GA, sixdalestrail.org.uk | Getting there Bus X 84, X 85 or 874 towards Otley; by car: take the A 660 out of the city centre towards Headingley and Bramhope before reaching Otley | Hours Accessible 24 hours | Tip Walkers can get a good rest by staying at Scaife Hall Farm at Blubberhouses, a working sheep farm near to the start (or finish) of the trail. It is a lovely farmhouse with great views and offers bed and breakfast to hikers.

90 — The Skyliner

Fish and chips fit for a lioness?

A lion walks into a local chippy. Far-fetched I hear you cry! But you would be wrong, as this is indeed what happened long ago in the Skyliner at Whitkirk. The story still resonates today at this long-established family fish and chip takeaway and restaurant nestled off the Selby Road. It has been 58 years now since the first hungry customers formed an orderly queue, and it remains highly popular in spite of competing with the more globally known Harry Ramsden's, also first founded in Leeds, but no longer domestically owned.

Olga, a circus lion tamer, used to be a regular customer at the Skyliner and would often be seen accompanied by her glamorous assistant, Elsa, a lioness with a love for the fragrant vinegary smell of battered Icelandic haddock resting on a bed of chunky chips. Luckily, Elsa preferred the Skyliner fayre to customers' meat and bones, and today's tight health and safety laws have consigned any similar tales to the story blender.

One person who is still there to witness life since the birth of the Skyliner, is its founder and owner, Johnny Meehan, who later handed the fish fryer on to son David and daughter-in-law, Elaine. These days, grandson Alvin and wife Sam are at the helm of the good ship Skyliner, employing more than 20 staff, including Jean who has served there for 23 years.

The story began in 1962 when Donegal-born Johnny spotted a niche in the market, observing that local pubs closed at 10pm leaving people bereft of further socialising. He promptly bought and built his business, naming it Skyliner, and it still stands on its original plot. Johnny's wife, Ellen, suggested the name, which was inspired by a trip to New York.

The Skyliner has moved with the times to welcome dishes for vegans and those with food intolerances. There's seating now too, providing customers with a sit down, a sing-song and a tipple in the restaurant.

Address 15 Austhorpe View, LS15 8NN, +44 (0)113 264 6853, www.theskyliner.co.uk |
Getting there Bus X 26 or 163 to Crossgates; by car: head towards Garforth on the Selby
Road B 6159 | Hours Mon & Tue 11.30am–8.30pm, Wed & Thu 11.30am–9pm, Fri
11.30am–10pm, Sat 11.30am–9pm, Sun noon–8.30pm | Tip St Mary's Church at
Whitkirk, which dates back to 1185, is a short walk away. Inside you can view the tomb
of local engineer, John Smeaton.

91 Slung Low

Offering culture for the masses

Founded in 2000, Slung Low is an award-winning theatre company based at the Warehouse in Holbeck and the Temple in Leeds, which has opened the door of opportunity to an undersung section of society whose voices are often ignored.

It is a charity that offers an interesting melting pot of live theatre and comedy performances, group talks, family festivals, kids' clubs, choirs and education. Both of these venues offer space and theatre equipment to other artists and community groups. In 2020, along with Leeds People's Theatre, they branched out into film-making and released their short movie, "The Good Book".

There is no hoity toity 'luvvie' behaviour here, for it has opened doors literally and metaphorically to the predominantly working-class residents in this south Leeds suburb and beyond. Everyone is welcome, and performances are on a 'pay what you think' basis, avoiding pricing out those on low incomes. 'A lot of people need this place,' explained Alan Lane, Artistic Director of Slung Low. Alan is a former military school alumnus who, with his trusty team, runs this charity with precision, endless good cheer and bags of enthusiasm. Slung Low was formerly housed in a room under the railway arches in Leeds but Alan, ever ambitious for the company to expand, found a permanent home in Holbeck.

The award-winning company also takes the show on the road and produces performances for the likes of the Royal Shakespeare Company; theatre groups can also hire out equipment. The newly acquired community double-decker bus enables Slung Low to reach out to local communities and carries the choir to sing for those who have difficulties travelling. Through its community college, it offers classes as diverse as boxing for beginners, the art of breadmaking, street photography, performance skills, writing, ukulele and stage combat.

Address The Holbeck, Jenkinson Lawn, Holbeck, LS11 9QX, +44 (0)7305 155698, info@slunglow.org, www.slunglow.org | Getting there Bus 54, 65 or 75 to Top Moor Side | Hours Check the website for times of performances and classes, but the building is open Mon, Wed, Fri & Sat 9am – 11.30pm, Sun 11.30am – 11.30pm | Tip The Matthew Murray Trail is a walk through Holbeck to Leeds Railway Station, taking in the rich heritage, including the former Holbeck Free Public Library, Marshalls Mill, the Round Foundry and the stunning Tower Works, a dominant Leeds landmark on Globe Road.

92 Sound Leisure

Jukeboxes fit for a princess

There is something special about a jukebox. With just the push of a button or two, it releases a little window to stored memories of pivotal moments in life through the prism of bubble tubes, diamond lights and solid oak. Alan Black is thought to be only one of two people in the world to make these wonderful treasures, which can be admired at his showroom in Crossgates. Princess Anne is one admirer; she even popped in to have a look in 2019.

Alan founded Sound Leisure in 1978 after years of tinkering and mending gadgets for mates. It was one of those lightbulb moments, and he decided he would handcraft his own jukeboxes and try to persuade people to buy. He initially shared his plan with the bank, only to be told it was a foolish 'candyfloss' idea. So it was a 'no' then; but the road to success, as they say, is invariably littered with a few failures along the way, and tenacity paid off as a friend who owed him a few favours, came to the rescue. Alan opened his factory, initially making pub jukeboxes, but the rising popularity of CDs led to him unveiling the first digital box in the 1980s. Despite a gloomy, public forecast that it was death to vinyl, Alan carried with him a sort of sixth sense about its future. It was merely sleeping – recharging the old batteries – before waking up; so he started crafting vinyl records again, and the results have figuratively and literally paid off.

The jukeboxes are in demand all over the world from folk with a bob or two to spare who just want to listen at home, to multi-billion pound conglomerates. Success hasn't turned his head, as Alan was keen to keep it a family-run business with his sons Mike and Chris. The boxes are essentially made in a traditional way, but customers request designs of their choice, on the front. The traditional Wurlitzer 1015 appears popular. Did the Princess Royal buy? She was 'very nice'.

Address Sandleas Way, LS15 8AR, +44 (0)113 232 1700, www.soundleisure.com | Getting there Bus 56, 64 or X27 to Sandleas Way; by car: York Road (A64) out of the city then A6129, turn left into Austhorpe Road, Manston Lane and turn right at Sandleas Way | Hours Mon–Fri 9am–5.30pm, Sat by appointment only | Tip The family-run, Wilson's Butchers on nearby Austhorpe Road, sells award-winning pork pies and takeaway bacon sandwiches.

93 South Entrance Leeds Railway Station

A heavenly world underneath the arches

If you are visiting Leeds for the first time, turn far away from the madding crowd in the city's railway station and head for the Holbeck Urban Village exit. Visitors will be guaranteed a lovely surprise.

The South Entrance – as it is also known – takes you under the beautifully kaleidoscopic colours of the Victorian railway arches to an underground world of fast-flowing waters of the Aire and Calder and canal locks. Once you have marvelled at the waterside rainbow spectacular, turn towards the sound of socialising folk frequenting the trendy bars, hotels and multi-cultural restaurants that pepper the neighbouring piazza. This rejuvenated area of Leeds, once an industrial wasteland, is now a major heavenly hub ready and willing to receive its visitors.

Opened in 2016, the south entrance is framed with a thoughtfully designed dome that would not be out of place at the Eden Project in Cornwall. Putting its steel structure in place was a challenge, as most of the construction was largely completed by workers on barges hoisting the metal from the adjacent waterway. The result was worth it, as it is adorned with windows aplenty to make the best of the views standing before it.

First-time visitors to Leeds may miss this spectacular gateway unless they know better. Only as little as 20 years ago, wheelchair and pushchair users together with bag-laden weary passengers had to call for assistance to help them make their way out of the station via the tired old service lift. Now escalators and lifts are rightfully in their place along with the conventional stairs.

One word of warning though: on the stroke of 10pm, the doors will be locked until 6am the following morning when the magic begins once again.

Address New Station Street, LS1 4DY | Getting there Buses run through the city centre to Leeds Railway Station; get off at Boar Lane | Hours Daily 6am – 10pm | Tip Just outside the station at Bishopsgate, you will find The Scarbrough Hotel, known locally as 'Scarbrough Taps'. It was built on the site of an old medieval manor house and was named after Henry Scarbrough who was landlord from 1826. During the 1890s it was renamed The Scarbrough Hotel and talent nights used to take place there.

94 Squires Café Bar

Looking for adventures?

Where else could one sit blissfully with a mug of tea and a bacon butty, talking 'frames' and 'front forks' while catching the odd 'double axel' and 'triple salchow'? Squires Café Bar still offers comfort foods, but has slowly evolved from a compact milk bar into a motorcyclists' oasis – even sporting its own ice rink! People have been hopping on the saddle to this bikers' café for 66 years and it has attracted bike and car enthusiasts from all corners of the country: one couple even rode from Switzerland to join the crowds!

These days, Squires can be found splendidly isolated in a former pub, in safe hearing distance of Sherburn-in-Elmet. It was originally known as Squires Bradburys Milk Bar when it opened in 1954 in the heart of the village, but customers started arriving on two wheels in 1974 after motorcycle fanatics, Harry and Sue Weston, took ownership. The roads to the 'bikers' mecca' are woven into its tale of longevity, as Squires can be found off open country lanes, a handy pit stop away from the A1. This provides a dream of a journey for most who do not consider a 300-mile road trip after a long day at work to be a huge problem. They gather at Squires in absolute hordes – weekends especially – to share knowledge, ideas, stories and, sadly, a few tragic memories that these speed machines can sometimes bring.

The milk bar eventually grew too big for the boots of the bikers' and in 2002 it moved to the present, Newthorpe site, leaving space to grow. The Westons retired in 2007, handing over to the Bowness family, and today hot beverages can be swapped for the stronger stuff as tent and caravan pitches are now provided for a bit of a 'rest'. These outdoor sleepover facilities could soon be joined by the greater comfort of bed and breakfast rooms. The pub and café juxtapose nicely with the dance floor and ice rink where you might just catch the beat of *Born to be Wild*.

Address Newthorpe Lane, Newthorpe, LS25 5LX, +44 (0)1977 684 618, www.squires-cafe.co.uk | Getting there Bus 402 or 403 to Selby to just before the railway bridge on Newthorpe Lane; by car: take the A 1(M), from there, head on to the B 1217 towards Lotherton, then follow the signs for the village of Sherburn, turn right into Sherburn and head out on to Newthorpe Lane | Hours Mar–Nov Mon–Fri 9am–10pm, Sat & Sun 8am–10pm; Nov–Mar Mon 1am–4pm, Tue 10am–10pm, Wed & Thu 9am–10pm, Fri 10am–8pm, Sat & Sun 8am–8pm | Tip Speedstyle is a separate entity to Squires but can be found in the far end of the car and bike park. It sells all types of motorcycle clothing and accessories, and also offers a bike maintenance service.

95 St George's Fields
A favourite with Leeds' Goths

St George's Fields is an esoteric place that is off the radar to many – even most locals – but it is a perfect green retreat, hiding away to greet the seekers who will be rewarded when they find it.

It is now a public space close to Leeds' two main university buildings, but between 1835 and 1969 it was Leeds General Cemetery and was open to all denominations wishing to inter their loved ones or scatter their ashes here. Overcrowding and public funding were the main reasons for its closure, and many of the headstones and tombs were moved when it opened as a leafy park in 1969. The attractive, pillared chapel still remains, and work has been carried out to ensure the records of the departed are kept alive. Some headstones are peppered here and there, but the place has a calm, renaissance feel to it and is a haven for wildlife and biodiversity studies.

St George's Fields has been a favourite meeting place for law-abiding groups of Goths who come to worship this sacred ground, as it was frequented by many of the Leeds-formed Gothic rock bands such as The Mission, March Violets, Salvation and Ghost Dance. But it is best known as the spot where Andrew Eldritch and his band, The Sisters of Mercy, were photographed for their album *First and Last and Always*. Eldritch was a student living around the corner from St George's Fields during the early 1980s, and is still adored by many Goths who perform their trademark 'two and a half steps to the front and back again' shuffle, while listening to the Sisters, tracks. These days, Eldritch refutes that his band was ever indeed part of the Goth movement, but die-hard fans refuse to exclude Sisters music from their collection. Pablo Fanque, the first person of colour to become a circus owner, is referenced in a line from the Beatles 'Being for the Benefit of Mr. Kite'! He died in 1871 and his grave still remains here.

Address St George's Fields, Woodhouse Lane, LS2 9JT | **Getting there** Bus 1, 6, 28 or 28A to University of Leeds and walk to the rear of the campus; the park is opposite Woodhouse Moor and Hyde Park | **Hours** Accessible 24 hours | **Tip** Goth City Promotions organises biannual trips to the home of the Goths (Leeds excepted) – Whitby. Goth City Promotions also puts on all things Goth in and around Leeds, including live concerts and talks.

96 St Mary's Chapel
A beauty standing in splendid isolation

If only walls could talk … one would suspect this pretty little ancient chapel could hold more secrets on its rich history than its 18-foot (5.5-metre) capacity could possibly allow.

St Mary's Chapel, also known as the Lead Chapel, was built in the mid-1400s and was part of a larger church constructed for use by the Tyas family, who were wealthy land owners in this particular part of Yorkshire. Historians say it is highly likely that St Mary's also provided a temporary refuge for soldiers fighting in the nearby Battle of Towton, in 1461, one of the bloodiest battles in the Wars of the Roses, a conflict between the Houses of Lancaster and York. It now stands in splendid isolation in a field close to the village of Saxton with only the grazing sheep and the Crooked Billet pub across the road for company. Another neighbour is Cock Beck, and legend has it the water ran a ruby red colour with the blood of men injured or dying in the Towton Battle, which claimed 10,000 lives.

Enter the creaking timber door, the chapel is beautifully presented thanks to local volunteers who keep a watchful eye over it and regularly dress it with floral delights on behalf of its owners, the Churches Conservation Trust. Its preserved pulpit and benches are early and late medieval pieces, respectively, and the walls speak out with ancient biblical texts, a deliberate reminder for visitors to mind their ps and qs perhaps? Today, it is a picture of peace and tranquillity for visitors from far and wide, and is especially popular with local walkers needing a bit of a sit down and some divine inspiration. It was actually rescued from decay during the 1930s by ramblers, and is also known as the 'Ramblers' Church'. Regular services may no longer take place, but it is a highly sought after location for film and television, and has been featured in the period dramas *Dark Angel* and *Victoria*.

Address Saxton, LS25 9QN, +44 (0)845 303 2760, www.visitchurches.org.uk | Getting
there Bus 843 to Stutton Road, then bus 492 at The Jackdaw to Scarthingwell Crescent,
then it is a 15-minute walk to the chapel; by car: take the A64 from the city centre towards
Tadcaster, then A1 (M) south and turn off for the B1217 towards Towton | Hours
Accessible 24 hours | Tip The Crooked Billet across the road on the B1217 offers not just
delicious pub meals, but further information on the chapel and the Battle of Towton can
also be discovered through their own literature on display.

97 St Paul's House

A palace for factory workers

Any Loiner returning to Leeds after a long period away will be surprised to discover a glorious, rather flamboyant-looking building, peeping over the concrete crowns of Leeds' business quarter.

St Paul's House is a marvellous example of Hispano-Moorish architecture, which is a hybrid of Spanish/Portuguese and North African design and it shows, especially on its ornate top floor and roof. The design character of St Paul's – grandly looking out onto the equally impressive Georgian, Park Square – is a sort of *doppelgänger* of London's St Pancras railway station.

Built in 1878, it is believed to be the first fully designed factory of its kind, and boasted cutting and pressing rooms housing around 200 sewing machines. It was designed by Leeds architect, Thomas Ambler, for Sir John Barran, pioneer of the ready-made clothing trade and a one-time Mayor of Leeds and Liberal MP for Otley.

A religious man with a social conscience, Barran believed in pleasant working conditions for his employees, equalled by good pay, which helped boost profits. With business booming at St Paul's, Barran expanded his firm in the city's Boar Lane, before branching out nationally with premises in London.

St Paul's has undergone a huge transformation over the years since the last stitch by Barran's crew was sewn, with nips and tucks here and there on the minarets and window arches. The roof has been given a radical face-lift to show off the ornate corner tower in white and terracotta. The cherry on the top comes in the form of a glass flat roof that works surprisingly well with the original Victorian design.

The five-floor house was sold for a reasonable £23.7 million in 2016 and Sedulo, 'financial consultants to entrepreneurs', has opened a Great Gatsby-themed champagne bar in its slice of the building, for customers. But would Barran and Ambler have approved?

Address 23 Park Square, LS1 2ND, +44 (0)113 235 1362 (general reception) | Getting there A short walk from Leeds Rail Station. Head towards Wellington Street before turning towards King Street and East Parade. | Hours Viewable from the outside only; bar by arrangement | Tip Sesame café around the corner on St Paul's Street is a lovely vegan and vegetarian deli and café that sells delicious wholemeal foods.

98_ Station House Café and Bistro

Bellissimo mamma!

Former station houses can often be found on much-lamented disused railway lines, the majority of which were closed under the wielding axe of Lord Beeching in the 1960s. The Leeds to Selby line was spared in the cost-cutting move and a regular supply of trains make their scheduled stop at Garforth Station. The 1873 station house – standing on the platform to Leeds – has morphed from 'old Tom's' house and ticket office, into a slice of Italian joy, as it is now an intimate restaurant run with a big heart.

The Station House Café and Bistro is run by Anglo-Italian husband and wife team Jo and Luigi Baranelli – her being a local girl and he hailing from Puglia on the heel of Italy's boot. The two met after Luigi moved to the UK in 1983, and decided to open this little café in the station house in 2016. They have now expanded their menu and opening times to include home-made dishes. Luigi makes all the authentic cuisine from scratch and Jo provides a warm welcome front of house. What makes this place special – food and cheerfulness apart – is that the couple have provided a perfectly laid family table on the first floor, especially for customers living with autism and other sensory challenges. Over the years, Jo had observed friends struggling in crowded, noisy restaurants and wanted to provide families with an evening out in their own home-from-home space.

The café is open at lunchtimes for hot and cold drinks, homemade cakes, and meals such as 'Baranelli's Breakfast', but now reopens in the evening with a more ambitious list of delicious Italian pasta and fish dishes, such as exotically named merluzzo pomodoro, all accompanied by Luigi's ciabatta bread. He makes a mean pizza too, with a vast range of toppings. Vegetarian, vegan and gluten-free delights are also available.

Address 1 Station House, Station Road, Garforth, LS25 2QQ, +44 (0)113 286 6322, www.thestationhousecafe.co.uk | **Getting there** Bus 19, 19A, 163 or 166 to Garforth Station; by train: take the Leeds to Hull or Leeds to Selby train | **Hours** Tue–Fri noon–2pm & 6–10pm, Sat 8am–2pm & 6–10pm | **Tip** A short walk away at Garforth Cliff is the former home of 1961 football pools winner, Viv Nicholson, who was famous for coining the phrase 'spend, spend, spend'. A book, play and musical about her hold the same titles, and she appeared on the front cover of The Smiths' single 'Heaven Knows I'm Miserable Now'.

99 Stourton Stone Circle

A mini Stonehenge for pagans

It resembles a 'mini me' version of Stonehenge, but unlike the Wiltshire Neolithic monument, no corner of Stourton Stone Circle has forbidden public access.

Standing on open rural ground close to Thwaite Mills Museum, Stourton Stone Circle provides a free visitor attraction, a picnic ground and – significantly – a place for pagan worshippers to meet and celebrate the eight Sabbats or seasonal celebrations. It was built by Tony Douglass on reclaimed land at Stourton in 1997 and the mystical solar creatures on the larger stones were sculpted by Melanie Wilks, a well-known artist and sculptor in Leeds.

Few ancient stone circles exist in Northern England but remains of some are reported to have been found in nearby Rothwell and Carlton. However, the Stourton monument is the only complete circle for pagan worship in the area. The significance of the circular shape is a deliberate, mirroring of the infinite cycle of nature, as the seasons never really end; rather they disappear but reappear later. Pagans apply the same principle after the passing of humans and reincarnation is a firmly held belief.

Leodis Pagan Group members from Leeds are the main frequent visitors to the circle, which consists of differing sized stones with a centre point in the form of a three-stone monument. Leodis help maintain the site along with the Rivers and Canal Trust and Leeds City Council. Paganism is an ancient worship of nature and the movement of the sun, which sparks the changing seasons. It holds a heavy ethos of equality, respect and friendship in one another and revolves around positive thinking. Debra Scott, a member of Leodis Pagans, helps organise the four major Sabbat meetings of the year, which largely coincide with season changes. Samhain Sabbat (Hallowe'en) is the most prominent visually as pagans usually dress the part in spooky costumes to honour loved ones' spirits.

Address Thwaite Mill, Thwaite Lane, Stourton, LS10 1RP | Getting there Bus 167, 168 or 189 to Stourton; by car: take the A 639 Pontefract road from Leeds city centre | Hours Accessible 24 hours | Tip Just across from the stone circle is a brand new stylish boathouse opened in 2014. It is owned by Leeds Rowing Club and University of Leeds Boat Club and has direct access to the waters of the Aire and Calder Navigation. Spectators or putative members are welcome.

100 — Sunny Bank Mills

Its light is shining after nearly 200 years

Anyone living in the pleasant vicinity of Sunny Bank Mills will probably count their blessings that such a magnificent, thriving gem sits right on their doorstep. The mill, nicely nestled in the heart of Farsley, is a glorious mixture of cultural activity, offering an art gallery, shops, cafés, artists' studios, a textile archive and museum, a weaving shed and workshops, and outdoor space. In 2022 it became the new home of the BBC's popular programme *The Great British Sewing Bee*.

In the summer of 2023, it welcomed the Post-16 department of the West Leeds Specialist Inclusive Learning Centre (SILC) to its Mending Rooms, to teach young people skills for specific job sectors.

Sunny Bank Mills rests on 10 acres of land and was once a leading global producer of worsted cloth. It first opened in 1829 as the Farsley Club Mill and was initially run by a co-operative team of clothiers. The name became Sunny Bank Mills in 1839 when the mill was owned by Roberts, Ross & Co. During World War I, the mill was expanded and taken over by wool tycoon Billy Gaunt, but during the Great Depression in 1929, ownership was handed over to the Inland Revenue and five major banks. Following Gaunt's death, his son Alfred rescued the mill from oblivion, and it thrived once more under the Gaunt family before production finally ceased in 2008.

Sunny Bank remains under the watchful eye of the Gaunts, courtesy of of cousins John and William. They sold the business itself due to pressures from a competitive market but kept the mill itself. After extensive renovations, Sunny Bank is now open to the public and home to around 100 independent creative businesses, creating nearly 500 jobs.

William salvaged a handful of 19th-century Dobby weaving looms, which have been painstakingly restored for demonstrations and teaching purposes. Sewing Bee judges, Esme and Patrick might decide to cast a critical eye!

Address 83-85 Town Street, Farsley, Pudsey LS28 5UJ, +44 (0)113 256 3239, www.sunnybankmills.co.uk, info@sunnybankmills.co.uk | Getting there Bus 16,72; train to Skipton, get off at Apperley Bridge and then it's a 16-minute walk; by car: take the Stanningley Bypass to Bradford Road, then the B6156 to Town Street | Hours See website for individual business' hours and events | Tip In nearby Pudsey, AW Hainsworth is a textile mill has been weaving cloth for 230 years. It is best known for producing the scarlet military cloth worn by the Royal most recently at the coronation of King Charles III in May 2023.

101 The Tetley

Raising a glass to Leeds' brewing past

Tetley's beer was synonymous with Leeds for nearly 200 years, and its trademark – the monocled huntsman raising a glass of beer – was once a ubiquitous sight on pub signs and walls in the city. But dwindling demand for the 'good stuff' led to last orders being called on its Hunslet Road headquarters, and production finally came to an end in 2011, leaving behind a significant and elegant reminder.

The Art Deco former brewery gatehouse was spared and renamed – though not so radically – as The Tetley. It formed a grand frontage to the more traditional brick offices and brewery buildings at Hunslet Road that were demolished in 2012. Carlsberg had merged with Tetley at this point and the high value of the land was partly blamed for the destruction and demise of production in Leeds. Tetley was swallowed by various other big brewing names in the wake of this. The gatehouse was built in 1931 and its original features, such as the intricate iron lift, stairway and ceilings, still remain, adding to the building's charm. A statue of the famous Tetley shire horses – another iconic symbol of the famous name – can be found next to the gatehouse. Shire horses were traditionally used to pull a tiny part of the produce up until 2006.

Today, The Tetley is an 'all-round entertainer' as it is now an art exhibition space and community hub, as well as housing a rustic bar and restaurant. Artefacts from its past, including bottled ales, are peppered around The Tetley, and information on its history is readily available.

William Tetley was already an established name in the early 1800s as a Leeds merchant of malt and spirits. He inspired his son, Joshua, to start his own brewing empire. Joshua bought a brewery in 1822 for just £400 and began operating at Salem Place in Hunslet. It was such a huge employer in the city, a whole regiment during World War I was made up of Tetley workers.

Address Hunslet Road, LS10 1JQ, +44 (0)113 320 2323, www.thetetley.org | Getting there On foot from Leeds Bus Station, cross over the River Aire via Brewery Wharf and continue to Hunslet Road or via Leeds Railway Station: cross Leeds Bridge and continue on to Hunslet Road. | Hours Restaurant and bar Mon & Tue 7.30am – 8pm, Wed – Fri 7.30am – 11pm, Sat 10am – 11pm, Sun 10am – 8pm; gallery open daily 10am – 5pm except Wed 10am – 8pm | Tip Salem Chapel, built in 1791, is the oldest surviving non-conformist chapel in Leeds and occupies part of the land where Tetley Brewery first started trading. Salem Chapel was also the first venue for a meeting to establish Leeds United Football Club in 1919, and a plaque was placed to commemorate this. Now private offices, it is not open to the general public.

102 Thackray Museum of Medicine

A necessary visit even for the faint-hearted

St James' – or 'Jimmy's' as it is known to locals - is the largest teaching hospital in Europe. Parts of the hospital date back to the Victorian era where more than 700 paupers in the city received care.

The splendid looking Leeds Union Workhouse, completed in 1861, now houses the Thackray Museum of Medicine. Opened in 1997, it is one of the largest medical museums in the UK and charts the history of disease and the development of treatments. Its founders were Paul Thackray, a medical supplies manufacturer, and the late Professor Monty Losowsky, a physician and educator. The award-winning museum, now run by a group of trustees who form a registered charity, offers displays, galleries, exhibitions, virtual tours, lectures, and films. Don't miss the 19th-century operating theatre, where blood-stained mannequins armed with saws and other horrific tools take visitors (via audio) through the grizzly amputation procedure that was used extensively at the time. It isn't for the faint-hearted, but it's a great way to educate and goes with gruesome good fun here!

Visitors get to walk down a model of a disease-ridden Victorian street in Leeds, but rest assured, it is safe to venture here. There is also a replica of an old apothecary shop. Children can enjoy and learn in an interactive space that seeks to inform them on the intricacies and inner workings of the human body. Mindful that museums like Thackray have a responsibility to tackle important and often taboo medical matters, there is also an area dedicated to sexual health.

In 2019, the museum closed for a £4 million redevelopment project. The pandemic delayed the opening, and the space fittingly became a temporary vaccine centre. It finally opened in 2021, with funding from the Culture Recovery Fund. The museum added a COVID-19 display of personal protective equipment and early vaccine samples.

Address 141 Beckett Street, Harehills, LS9 7LN, +44 (0) 113 244 4343, www.thackraymuseum.co.uk, info@thackraymuseum.co.uk | Getting there Bus 16, 42, 49, 50, 50A to St James's University Hospital; by car: an 8-minute drive from the city centre via the Wetherby/York Road, A 58 and A 64 | Hours Daily 10am–5pm | Tip Another historical building in the postal district of LS 8 at Gledhow Valley Woods, is the open-air bath house at Gipton Spa. Built in 1671, this is a Grade 2 listed building and was built on the orders of Edward Waddington, Lord of Gledhow Manor.

103 Thwaite Mills

The ancient wheel still keeps turning

Built in 1641, this beautifully restored mill has undergone a healthy plethora of identities during its time and is still enjoying a busy semi-retirement.

Sitting in its own island on the Aire and Calder Navigation – pedants can be satisfied with this accurate aquatic description – it is now a council-run museum showcased to the public thanks to a small team of enthusiasts along with Milly the cat. It also provides a lovely venue for weddings, school trips, vintage car shows and lots more after it was brought back to a rightful life thanks to efforts from the Thwaite Mills Society. After years in solitary confinement, it was given another lease of life and reopened in 1990.

The ancient water wheel – thought to be one of the oldest in the country – has, during its time, ground chalk, flint, china, stone, seed and wood. The Horn family took ownership of Thwaite in the 1870s and produced putty on a grand scale, which would prove especially vital during World War II. Putty was once a ubiquitous agent in the sealing of windows and doors. It was London's dwellings that took the bulk of the brunt in the Blitz bombings, and Thwaite Mills produced and dispatched hundreds of thousands of putty tins to patch up the destruction in the capital's shattered homes.

Steve Hutcheon, a former rock roadie for bands such as Queen, can be found upstairs in the learning centre at Thwaite imparting a mountain of information about the mill, as well as his former life with the giants of rock. In addition to guided tours and demonstrations of the mill and working engine shed, you can enter a Victorian house once owned by the Horns. It is dressed and furnished authentically as if the Horn family had just moved in. Visitors can also venture outdoors where several lovely orchards and nature trails illustrate the surrounding land, now a natural playground for returning wildlife.

Address Thwaite Lane, Stourton, LS10 1RP, +44 (0)113 214 191,
www.leeds.gov.thwaitemills | Getting there Bus 110, 189 or 444 to Pontefract Road/
Plevna Street | Hours Sat & Sun noon–4pm, Tue–Fri during school holidays
10am–5pm | Tip Just beyond the car park there is a lovely nature trail dedicated to the
memory of environmental scientist, Ben Walmsley, who worked nearby. It has sandstone
posts and has been created by Ben's family and friends.

104 The Tiled Hall

A happy end to an abandoned past

The Victorian Tiled Hall shines in the cultural spotlight after enduring a troubled past of neglect and abandonment. In its heyday, this most glorious of halls was once the reading rooms of Leeds Central Library, but it is now a grand tea room providing a watering hole for bookworms and visitors to the neighbouring Leeds art and sculpture galleries. It was brought to life in 2007 after being shamelessly hidden for nearly 50 years behind false walls, reference books, vaults and ceilings. Resurrecting the Tiled Hall was part of a huge restoration project at the library that led to the discovery of this hidden treasure. Most of the original features include the hall's marble columns and archway, the parquet floor and stunning mosaic ceiling, which were painstakingly recovered. The *pièce de résistance*, though, was the discovery of the hall's walls that were almost entirely cladded with the iconic Leeds Burmantofts decorative tiles.

Built in 1884 by George Corson, the stunning hall is dressed once again with some original and ornate replicas of the glazed Burmantofts tiles, once used as a glamorous coat on many houses, stations, pubs and public buildings during the late 19th and early 20th centuries. The Leeds-based Burmantofts Faience Factory – established in 1842 – produced globally renowned pottery and pressed fireclay tiles for floors, ceilings and walls. Burmantofts tiles were exported all over Britain and the globe until manufacturing finally ceased in 1957. The tiles have provided dashing façades and interiors to older pubs in Leeds including The Garden Gate in Hunslet and the City of Mabgate Inn as well as wider afield, such as the exterior of London's Chalk Farm Tube Station.

Reminders of the hall's literary roots are ever present next to the cream teas and the lattes as portraits of writers such as Milton and Keats provide good companions to the tiles.

Address The Headrow, LS1 3AB, +44 (0)113 535 1370 | Getting there Bus 14, 15, 19 or 19A to The Headrow; on foot, a 10-minute walk from Leeds Railway Station and 15-minute walk from Leeds Bus Station | Hours Mon–Sat 9am–5pm, Sun 11am–3pm | Tip Henry Moore's *Reclining Figure* sculpture stands just outside Leeds Art Gallery. Henry Moore (1898–1986) was born 10 miles from Leeds in the town of Castleford, and studied at Leeds School of Art. His sculptures can also be seen at Yorkshire Sculpture Park at Bretton, Wakefield.

105 Tolkien's Letters
A box of treasures for Tolkien fans

John Ronald Reuel Tolkien held a professorship at the University of Leeds during the 1920s and formed a firm friendship with one of his colleagues, Eric Gordon. It is thanks to Professor Gordon's family that a tangible reminder of the author's time in the city is preserved.

By prior appointment, you can delve gingerly into a fascinating box of handwritten letters by Tolkien – author of *The Lord of the Rings* trilogy – to the Gordons. There are also some original handwritten compositions of poems and songs, including 'The Homecoming of Beorhtnoth Beorhthelm's Son' in pencil and ink. But Tolkien's work is extensive and it might take a huge chunk out of your day to absorb all the contents.

For many of Tolkien's fans, the box's showstopper will be one of the first editions of *The Hobbit*, signed by the author himself to Professor Gordon, his wife Ida, and their children. Slightly frayed and covered in green cloth, it includes Thror's map of Wilderland and was sent as a gift to coincide with the book's publication in 1937. For fans, handling this and the beautifully handcrafted work, is likely to be a huge privilege.

South African-born Tolkien (1892–1973) came to Leeds in 1920 to take up a position as reader in English language, becoming the youngest professor there. Much of his work in the city included research into literature written in Old Norse and English. Reports suggested he loved his time in Leeds as he even willingly joined the Yorkshire Dialect Society! He left six years later for a post at Oxford but during that time he struck up a lasting friendship with Canadian-born Professor Gordon who repeatedly advised Tolkien not to waste his time penning 'fairy stories'!

Professor Gordon's untimely death at the age of 42 was said to have left Tolkien devastated, despite the 'stiff upper lip' tone in a condolence letter to Ida which is included in the box.

Address Special Collections, Brotherton Library, University of Leeds, Woodhouse Lane, LS2 9JT, +44 (0)113 3343 6178, www.library.leeds.ac.uk | Getting there Bus 1, 6, 7 or 56 to Woodhouse Lane; on foot, it is a 20-minute walk from City Square | Hours By appointment only; contact Special Collections via the website | Tip Before you get to the Special Collections room, walk through and take a long look at the Brotherton Library, a beautiful Grade II-listed Beaux-Arts building named after Edward Brotherton, 1st Baron Brotherton, who donated funds for the library's construction.

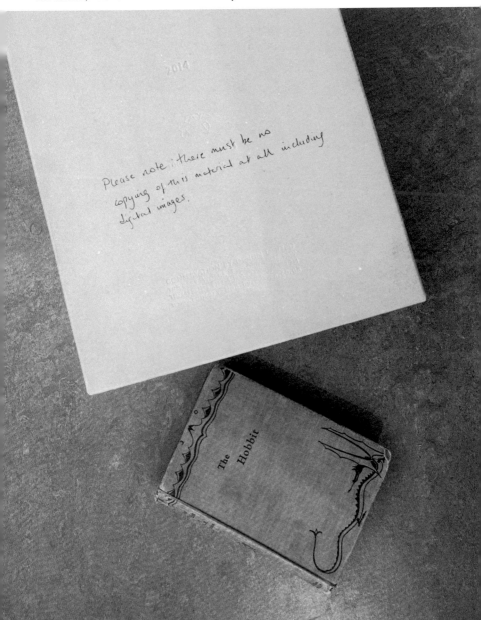

106 The Triumphal Arch

An American sympathiser in Parlington Woods

Surprises greet you around many corners in and around Leeds, and this little piece of 'Rome' in support of America is a real find.

The Triumphal Arch was once the gateway to the now demolished Parlington Hall standing in the middle of the luscious green grounds of the former Gascoigne-owned Parlington Estate, close to Aberford. It was designed by Thomas Leverton in 1781 for Sir Thomas Gascoigne, 8th Baronet, a member of the gentrified Gascoigne family who came to Yorkshire from Gascony in France. It was a rather lavish, visual display in support of the Americans who, at the time of construction, were fighting the War of Independence against the British from 1775 to 1783. The magnificent arch was built with the Roman structure, the Arch of Titus, in mind, but in reality its look has more in common with the Arch of Constantine near to the Colosseum in Rome. One theory is that Thomas Gascoigne's love of Roman architecture was sparked by a visit to the capital where he was given a papal pardon after being implicated in the death of a coachman. The original inscribed words – still clearly visible on the arch – read *Liberty in N. America Triumphant MDCCLXXXIII*. Legend has it that shortly after the arch was erected, a planned visit by The Prince of Wales was aborted after the Royal turned heel and rode the other way when he spotted the declaration of allegiance was for America and not Britain.

Thomas Gascoigne was born in Cambrai, Northern France, therefore sympathies with the Americans, whose cause was supported by the French, was understandable to some. He also echoed the thoughts of anti-war protestors in Parliament, wholly opposed to the conflict. However, he was branded 'treacherous' by many, for his pro-American views. Plans to move the arch to the States for the bicentenary celebrations of American Independence in 1976 were abandoned, following public protest.

Address The arch is accessible to the public from Cattle Lane off the Aberford to Barwick-in-Elmet Road, LS25 3EH | Getting there Bus 64 to Cattle Lane; by car: take the A 64 York Road from the city centre and drive through Barwick before turning into Potterton Lane and Long Lane | Hours Accessible 24 hours | Tip Parlington Woods is now a place of special interest after being protected from development by being recognised in the Historic Parks and Gardens list. It is a lovely place to walk and picnic. Rumour has it there is a secret underground labyrinth somewhere on the estate that comprises subterranean corridors leading to the house.

107__ *Twee* and *Drie*
Whatever happened to number one?

You can't tell the sisters apart … save for the names *Twee* and *Drie* on their little yellow sides. Two identical little tug boats were brought over from Amsterdam, hence their names – Dutch for 'two' and 'three'. They were surplus to requirements in the Netherlands, but much needed in Leeds, which lacked any sort of visitor boat. Two entrepreneurs wanted to show off a rejuvenated waterfront, inaccessible and dingy in previous years, but not anymore.

They were the vision of local businessmen from Allied London, determined to hold a mirror up to innovation along the River Aire, which was pretty much hidden away with embarrassment until recently. Initially, the 12-minute taxi ride was provided entirely free, but a £1 charge was introduced in the summer of 2019 (although children still travel free). Four part-time musicians are employed to captain the boat in glorious turns: Richard, Simon, Chris and Richard drive up and down from Granary Wharf to Leeds Dock seven days a week between them, and they have tales aplenty from the riverbank to impart.

In March 2019, chugging up the river was halted briefly to allow experts to take away an unexploded World War II bomb, discovered by an unsuspecting magnet fisherman, but thankfully these dramas are a rarity, and passenger safety is assured. Local and international visitors can usually enjoy the tranquil spot away from the bustle of the city, which has welcomed back to the water wildlife such as otter, kingfisher, grebe and heron, and you can hop off at Leeds Dock, home to a plethora of digital and tech companies. But the special attractions around the dock are museums, Leeds Discovery Centre and Royal Armouries.

The lads are happy to talk about their music along the journey and to impart their extensive knowledge of the city. They are laid-back free thinkers, but one question has yet to be answered: whatever happened to number 1?

Address Taxis can be boarded at Leeds Dock (by the Royal Armouries) and Granary Wharf (South Entrance of Station) | Getting there Walk to the lock bridge in front of Bar Brasil when embarking at Granary Wharf | Hours Mon–Fri 7am–7pm, Sat & Sun 10am–6pm | Tip There is a towpath running from Leeds Dock, heading south of the city, which you can take to spot a huge ongoing climate innovation project with sustainable houses, bridges, apartments and green spaces.

108_ The Warehouse

Leeds' answer to New York's CBGBs

The Warehouse has remained an important venue on the music club scene for more than 40 years, and it all started at the hands of a former American spy. Nebraskan Mike Wiand worked as an agent for the American government and was stationed in North Yorkshire after a spell in Russia. He fell in love with the county, making it his adopted home, and bought a disused warehouse in the quiet, cobbled, Somers Street in 1979. The Warehouse was one of the first in the country to introduce techno and dance music, and it quickly became a magnet for club goers from all over the UK who moved to numbers mixed at the hands of reputable DJs such as Greg James and Danny Pucciarelli. The club also showcased live music and it provided a stage for up-and-coming 1980s bands making their debuts such as Frankie Goes to Hollywood, The Stone Roses and Depeche Mode.

However, it was one former Leeds art student who remains synonymous with The Warehouse. Marc Almond, a sometime DJ and cloakroom attendant at the club, performed a memorable Warehouse gig with his college mate David Ball. The song was a cover version of Gloria Jones' 'Tainted Love'. Marc didn't need to return to his job after the performance, as the song went on to launch the career of his band, Soft Cell.

Throughout the 1980s and 1990s, The Warehouse continued to attract the cool and the famous, counting rock gods such as Iggy Pop and The Ramones among its illustrious list of drop-in guests, and although it is now the 'granddaddy' of the bright young venues of Leeds' present club scene, it has reinvented itself over the years. It is now a club for art sound and rave music and continues to feature live acts.

It endured a sabbatical in 2010, but reopened its doors three years later when a loyal group of music lovers took over the decks. Mike Wiand died in 2014, aged 70, and many in the city gave grateful thanks for his legacy.

Address 19–21 Somers Street, LS1 2RG, +44 (0)113 426 5078, www.thewarehouseleeds.com | Getting there Bus 5, 19 or 72 to Leeds Town Hall; by car: take the Westgate / Headrow turn off on Leeds' Inner Ring Road | Hours Wed, Fri & Sat 11pm–early hours | Tip Around the corner from Somers Street, at 33 Park Square, is the house that once belonged to pioneering abdominal surgeon, Sir Berkeley Moynihan (1865–1936). Sir Berkeley was credited with saving hundreds of lives at the Western Front in France during World War I.

109 Wharf Chambers

DIY venue where bouncers need not apply

Wharf Chambers is a workers' co-operative initiative, functioning on an 'everybody mucks in' basis, which was founded by a group of left-wing thinkers, striving to make equality count. It is a no-frills sort of a place but has charm and ambience when the music starts to play. The stage is mostly occupied by young (and sometimes old) punk or post-punk bands and grunge musicians.

Wharf also provides low-cost space for language classes, workshops, discussion collectives, and the co-op members actively seek out minority groups to spread the message that it is a place wholly dedicated to inclusivity. Wharf prides itself on never needing the services of a burly bouncer to control loutish behaviour, as ne'er-do-wells are never part of the clientele.

Located in a former pork pie factory in The Calls district of Leeds, the chambers is an offshoot of The Common Place, which was a social centre, born out of an anti-capitalist, anti-racist and anti-globalisation school of thought. Similarly, Wharf Chambers follows suit, and was the brainchild of Paul, Nick, Susan, Andrew, Keir and their friends, seven years ago. Social centres like Wharf, The Cowley in Brighton and The Trades Club in Hebden Bridge, were set up to mirror the mood of anti-capitalists wanting to voice an alternative view to that of the corporate giants. Profits made from annual membership fees – just one pound per person – are put into the pot needed for running costs, and Paul and Co. fit time in between jobs and studying to share the responsibilities of cleaning, maintenance work, sound engineering at gigs, staffing the doors and running the bar.

Mindful that most of the founding members do not fall into the minority category, the co-operative holds regular meetings to address the issue of a welcome space for all and publishes reports on their efforts to achieve their inclusivity goals.

Address 23–25 Wharf Street, LS2 7EQ, +44 (0)7523 307 089, www.wharfchambers.org | Getting there Bus 5, 19, 19A, 40 or 47 to Kirkgate, then a 10-minute walk to Wharf Street | Hours Membership required to attend events, but this is readily granted (takes 48 hours to start); Mon–Wed 5pm–midnight, Thu 5pm–1am, Fri 5pm–2am, Sat 3pm–2am, Sun 3–10pm | Tip One of the founding members of Wharf Chambers, Professor Paul Chatterton, is the co-founder of LILAC, a low-cost, low-impact eco housing development in Bramley, Leeds. Residents manage the homes and land as members of a Mutual House Ownership Society, and you can visit the eco site and admire the gardens.

110 __ Whitelocks Ale House

'The very heart of Leeds' (Betjeman)

Step off bustling Briggate into an ancient yard and you enter a little inner sanctum from frantic city life. On the left occupying the loin – essentially a yard – you will find the city's oldest and most famous of pubs, Whitelocks.

What is a loin? Many of Leeds' oldest pubs such as The Angel and The Ship, can be found down similar backyards, and they are historically known as 'loins', which gave way to the term 'loiner', a name for a native of Leeds (see ch. 53).

Today, Whitelocks is now joined by the Turk's Head pub, but essentially they are the same, and both come under the watchful eye of present proprietor, Ed Mason. Established in 1715, this most ancient of pubs has hardly changed in appearance. It was a regular haunt for poet John Betjeman when he visited the city and Hunslet-born writer, novelist and columnist, the late Keith Waterhouse. King George V's son, the Duke of Kent, once had part of the pub curtained off to hold a royal party because he liked it so much.

The pub – originally known as Whitelock's First City Luncheon Bar – was rebuilt and run by the Whitelock family during the 1800s, and in 1897 it was thought to be the first place in Leeds to have electricity installed. At the time, a revolving search light was placed by John Lupton Whitelock on the Briggate entrance beckoning patrons to ensconce themselves for a pint. Many of the original features from the 1800s remain, such as the long marble-topped bar, etched mirrors and the stained-glass partitions.

Today, hearty fayre is good accompaniment to the many local and craft beers on offer. One can devour Sunday roasts complete with Yorkshire pudding and comforting pie and mash, though salad is a worthy option. Patrons can also soak up the atmosphere from the outside as – thanks to the loin – you can suspend disbelief that you are in the city and imagine you are sitting outside a Yorkshire country pub.

Address Turk's Head Yard, LS1 6HB, +44 (0)113 245 3950, www.whitelocksleeds.com | Getting there Buses run through the city centre and you can get off at The Trinity (shopping centre) on Boar Lane. From the front of the train station, turn right and walk towards the Corn Exchange. On reaching Briggate, turn left and Whitelocks is just after the Marks and Spencer store on the left | Hours Mon–Thu 11am–midnight, Fri & Sat 11–1am, Sun 11am–11pm | Tip You will find another historic pub at 3 Whitfield Place, Hunslet. The Garden Gate, built in 1902, is now a Grade II-listed building. It was saved from demolition and has now been described as Leeds' most beautiful pub by CAMRA members. The interior has stained-glass windows, oak panels and tiled floors, many of which were salvaged during renovations.

111 Yorkshire County Cricket Club Museum

Where dreams just might come true

There is something rather special about the hallowed cricket ground at Headingley. The 'Botham and Willis test match' in 1981 springs to mind with that momentous victory over the Aussies. Or could this have been usurped in August 2019, when Ben Stokes grabbed an incredible victory in a last wicket stand with Jack Leach in the third Ashes test?

These moments in cricketing history here go back a lot further of course, and they are recounted in this compact museum at Yorkshire County Cricket Club's ground, which comes to life on home match days, but gladly opens for small group tours throughout the year. So many illustrious alumni have played for the county, they alone could fill the *Wisden Cricketers' Almanack*, and the museum is inevitably packed with all the relevant facts and artefacts about the game in 'God's Own Country'.

From its inception at Sheffield's Adelphi Hotel in 1863 to the present day, the museum traces the history of the club, and a special mention is given to Lord Hawke, who was appointed Yorkshire team captain in 1883. He initially dismissed his men as 'ten drunks and a parson', before reshaping them into one of the best sides in the country. The lives of the Yorkshire greats are rightly celebrated here, from Wilfred Rhodes to Joe Root via Hutton, Truman, Close, Illingworth, Boycott and Bairstow. There is also a small cinema showing films that namecheck the Yorkshire legends, and it is fitting that the incomparable Hedley Verity has his own pride of place as arguably the ultimate Yorkshire legend who died a hero during World War ll. When Hedley was hit by flying shrapnel, his final words to his comrades were 'keep going'. Perhaps on a perfect summer's day in 2019, he was looking down on Stokes and Leach, uttering those same words!

Address Emerald Headingley Cricket Stadium, Kirkstall Lane, LS6 3DP,
+44 (0)113 2033 665, www.yorkshireccc.com | Getting there Bus 6 to the cricket ground;
10-minute walk from Burley Park or Headingley train stations | Hours Group bookings
are possible via the website, and the museum opens during test and county home games |
Tip Just a stone's throw from the stadium is Welton Grove, where you can find Hedley
Verity's former home in which he was born. It is marked with a blue plaque: 'Hedley
Verity (1905–1943)'.

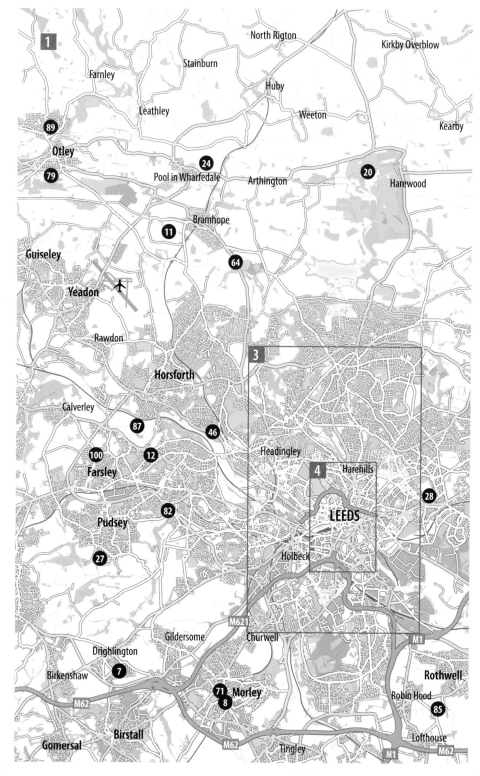

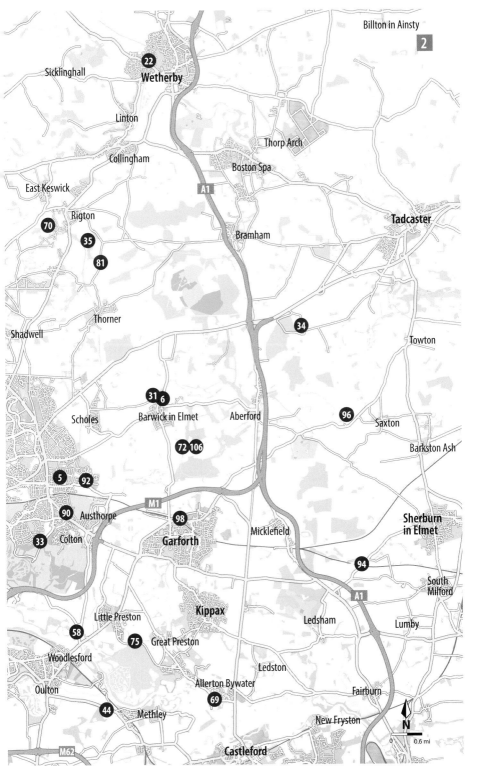

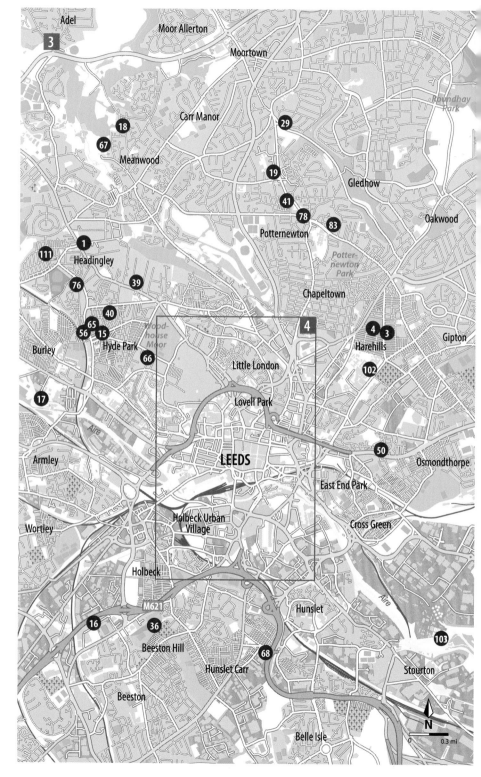

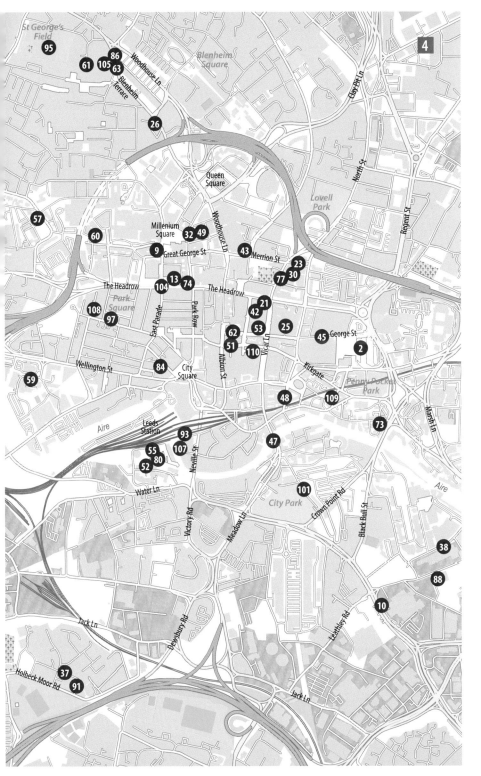

Julian Treuherz,
Peter de Figueiredo
111 Places in Manchester
That You Shouldn't Miss
ISBN 978-3-7408-1862-3

Julian Treuherz,
Peter de Figueiredo
111 Places in Liverpool
That You Shouldn't Miss
ISBN 978-3-7408-1607-0

Michael Glover,
Richard Anderson
111 Places in Sheffield
That You Shouldn't Miss
ISBN 978-3-7408-1728-2

Solange Berchemin
111 Places in the Lake District
That You Shouldn't Miss
ISBN 978-3-7408-1861-6

Katherine Bebo, Oliver Smith
111 Places in Poole
That You Shouldn't Miss
ISBN 978-3-7408-0598-2

Alexandra Loske
111 Places in Brighton and
Lewes That You Shouldn't Miss
ISBN 978-3-7408-1727-5

Tom Shields, Gillian Tait
111 Places in Glasgow
That You Shouldn't Miss
ISBN 978-3-7408-1863-0

Gillian Tait
111 Places in Edinburgh
That You Shouldn't Miss
ISBN 978-3-7408-1476-2

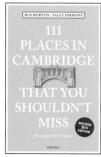

Rosalind Horton,
Sally Simmons, Guy Snape
111 Places in Cambridge
That You Shouldn't Miss
ISBN 978-3-7408-1285-0

Justin Postlethwaite
111 Places in Bath
That You Shouldn't Miss
ISBN 978-3-7408-0146-5

Frank McNally
111 Places in Dublin
That You Shouldn't Miss
ISBN 978-3-95451-649-0

John Sykes, Birgit Weber
111 Places in London
That You Shouldn't Miss
ISBN 978-3-7408-1644-5

Alexia Amvrazi,
Diana Farr Louis, Diane Shugart,
Yannis Varouhakis
111 Places in Athens
That You Shouldn't Miss
ISBN 978-3-7408-0377-3

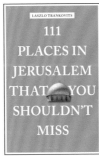

Laszlo Trankovits
111 Places in Jerusalem
That You Shouldn't Miss
ISBN 978-3-7408-0320-9

Kathleen Becker
111 Places in Lisbon
That You Shouldn't Miss
ISBN 978-3-7408-0383-4

Catrin George Ponciano
111 Places along the Algarve
That You Shouldn't Miss
ISBN 978-3-7408-0381-0

Andrea Livnat,
Angelika Baumgartner
111 Places in Tel Aviv
That You Shouldn't Miss
ISBN 978-3-7408-0263-9

Kay Walter, Rüdiger Liedtke
111 Places in Brussels
That You Shouldn't Miss
ISBN 978-3-7408-0259-2

Thomas Fuchs
111 Places in Amsterdam
That You Shouldn't Miss
ISBN 978-3-7408-0023-9

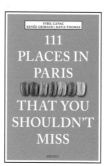

Sybil Canac, Renée Grimaud,
Katia Thomas
111 Places in Paris
That You Shouldn't Miss
ISBN 978-3-7408-0159-5

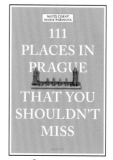

Matěj Černý, Marie Peřinová
111 Places in Prague
That You Shouldn't Miss
ISBN 978-3-7408-0144-1

Lucia Jay von Seldeneck,
Carolin Huder
111 Places in Berlin
That You Shouldn't Miss
ISBN 978-3-7408-0589-0

Annett Klingner
111 Places in Rome
That You Must Not Miss
ISBN 978-3-95451-469-4

Dirk Engelhardt
111 Places in Barcelona
That You Must Not Miss
ISBN 978-3-95451-353-6

Kai Oidtmann
111 Places in Iceland
That You Shouldn't Miss
ISBN 978-3-7408-0030-7

Jo-Anne Elikann
111 Places in New York
That You Must Not Miss
ISBN 978-3-7408-2057-2

Floriana Petersen, Steve Werney
111 Places in San Francisco
That You Must Not Miss
ISBN 978-3-7408-2058-9